How to Measure Social Media

A Step-by-Step Guide to Developing and Assessing Social Media ROI

NICHOLE KELLY

800 East 96th Street,
Indianapolis, Indiana 46240 USA

How to Measure Social Media: A Step-by-Step Guide to Developing and Assessing Social Media ROI

ISBN-13: 978-0-7897-4985-7
ISBN-10: 0-7897-4985-8

The Library of Congress cataloging-in-publication data is on file.

Printed in the United States of America

First Printing: October 2012

Trademarks

All terms mentioned in this book that are known to be trademarks or service marks have been appropriately capitalized. Que Publishing cannot attest to the accuracy of this information. Use of a term in this book should not be regarded as affecting the validity of any trademark or service mark.

Warning and Disclaimer

Every effort has been made to make this book as complete and as accurate as possible, but no warranty or fitness is implied. The information provided is on an "as is" basis. The author and the publisher shall have neither liability nor responsibility to any person or entity with respect to any loss or damages arising from the information contained in this book.

Bulk Sales

Que Publishing offers excellent discounts on this book when ordered in quantity for bulk purchases or special sales. For more information, please contact

U.S. Corporate and Government Sales
1-800-382-3419
corpsales@pearsontechgroup.com

For sales outside of the U.S., please contact

International Sales
international@pearson.com

TABLE OF CONTENTS

About the Author

Nichole Kelly is a pioneer in making social marketing efforts consistently profitable, measurable, and accountable. She is the president of SME Digital, the digital agency division of Social Media Explorer, and has worked for companies of all sizes, from Signs By Tomorrow-USA to Sherwin-Williams, Deutsche Bank Alex.Brown to The Federal Reserve Bank. Kelly runs the No-Fluff Social Media Measurement Boot Camp and has spoken at leading events including Dreamforce, B2B Summit, BlogWorld, Social Fresh, SocialTech, Inbound Marketing Summit, Exploring Social, Marketing Profs University, Small Business Success Summit, and the Social Media Success Summit. She writes about social media measurement for two of *Ad Age*'s top 30 marketing blogs, Social Media Examiner and Social Media Explorer.

Dedication

This book is dedicated to my three children, Huntor, Kaden, and Giavanna, and my amazing husband, Jason. Without them, life would not be complete.

Acknowledgments

Many people may not realize how much work it is to actually write a book. We naturally look to the author as the person who puts in the most time, but this process showed me that the support network of the author deserves the most praise.

As such, I'll start with my family. I'd like to thank my amazing husband, Jason Kelly, for giving me unending emotional support through this process. He is and always has been my biggest cheerleader and consistently tells me I can do anything I put my mind to. I love him with all my heart and could not have finished this book if he wouldn't have helped me manage the household while I had my head down busting out chapters. You are my rock, Jay!

My two boys, Huntor and Kaden, were amazingly supportive and understanding when I had to miss a lacrosse game, couldn't participate in family movie night, or even when I tried and fell asleep on the couch at 9 p.m. because I'd been up since 5 a.m. writing. They also think it's kind of cool that their mom wrote a book even if it is on a subject they may not understand yet. Many of you may not know that I undertook this project right after giving birth to my beautiful daughter, Giavanna. I was so blessed that she was such a happy baby who was easy to please. I don't know what I would've done if she would have had colic, couldn't sleep, or was generally miserable in her first year. Giavanna, I am so thankful that God brought you into our family and gave you such a wonderful disposition that made it possible to get this book completed on time.

I also had the support of my sister, Sarah, who helped watch the kids, did my laundry, and provided the occasional pat on the back when I needed it. I am also very thankful for my amazing in-laws, John and Jean Kelly. They are so supportive of everything we do and are two of the most amazing grandparents I've ever met. Their unconditional support and love was so appreciated. Jean has watched Giavanna during the day since she was five days old. I am so thankful that Giavanna was in such good hands while I was working on building a business during the day and writing a book on nights and weekends. Without her support and understanding, this book would not have been possible. While my own mother, Karen, doesn't live close by, she took the time to fly out and help with the kids when I needed it and has been such a great listener, supporter, and advocate for us. Thank you all for everything you have done to make this possible.

I'd also like to thank my colleagues. My business partner, Jason Falls, recommended me for this topic to Que and was completely honest about how much work it takes to produce a great book. I think his exact words were, "You may want to shoot yourself a few times throughout the process, but it will be worth it." Thank you for your honesty and for recommending me. Without your introduction, this book may never have made it off my computer screen and into bookstores. Katherine Bull, my acquisitions editor, is best-in-class. She made me feel like a rock star and walked me through everything step by step. She made sure all the pieces fell together while making it look so easy. Through the process, she became a great friend and confidant, and I'm so thankful to have met her. Matt Grant graciously offered to be the peer editor for this book to make sure the content was in line with what you would be looking for and that this book wasn't full of fluff. Thank you for taking your spare time to keep me in check and providing your insightful comments along the way.

I'd like to extend a special thank-you to Andrew Akers, who was a previous boss and is one of my greatest mentors. He has enough faith in me that he was officially the first person to preorder this book. You rock!

I'd also like to take the time to thank all the companies who participated and provided their stories so we could learn from them, including Joseph Manna from InfusionSoft, Rachel Sprung from HubSpot, Dan Moyle from AmeriFirst Mortgage, Brannan Atkinson from Raven Tools, Nan Dawkins from Social Snap, Albert Chou and Peter Heffring from Expion, Mandy Newgrosh from Tracx, and Eric Boggs from Argyle. And thank you to all the other tools that graciously gave me demos. I had to prioritize those that were included based on how much they aligned with the methodologies in this book, but there are some really great monitoring tools out there that are starting to get serious about measurement, too. I expect to see really great innovations in how metrics are presented in many of the tools available in the market over the next 18 months, so keep your eyes open. Thank you especially to Peter Heffring and Nan Dawkins who decided I might have something valuable to offer for their product road map and subsequently hired SME Digital to provide consulting on their products based on the early feedback I gave them during their demos.

Finally, I'd like to thank some of my early mentors who helped me get started in social media and provided tremendous insights and learnings and even took me under their wing when I was just a newbie. Without their guidance and acceptance, this book never would've been in the realm of possibility for me. Thank you to Carissa O'Brien, Greg Cangialosi, Amber Naslund, Ryan Holmes, C.C. Chapman, Chris Brogan, Tim Hayden, DJ Waldow, Tom Webster, Chris Penn, Mike Stelzner, Tamsen McMahon, Cindy King, Irene O'Leary, Justin Levy, David B. Thomas, Michael Brito, Marcus Sheridan, Derek Halpern, Zena Weist, Heather Whaling, Dharmesh Shah, Giovanni Cavalieri, Joel Witt, Antonia Dodge, Amber Osborne, and Jeff Pulver.

Thank you to all of my fans and followers who make me look awesome every time you share my content. Thank you to everyone who reached out to me over the years. So many of you have become great friends through Twitter, Facebook, and LinkedIn. Thank you to anyone and everyone who has supported me along the way.

You are all awesome. Now let's rock some awesome together and start measuring what matters.

We Want to Hear from You!

As the reader of this book, *you* are our most important critic and commentator. We value your opinion and want to know what we're doing right, what we could do better, what areas you'd like to see us publish in, and any other words of wisdom you're willing to pass our way.

We welcome your comments. You can email or write to let us know what you did or didn't like about this book—as well as what we can do to make our books better.

Please note that we cannot help you with technical problems related to the topic of this book.

When you write, please be sure to include this book's title and author as well as your name and email address. We will carefully review your comments and share them with the author and editors who worked on the book.

Email: feedback@quepublishing.com

Mail: Que Publishing
ATTN: Reader Feedback
800 East 96th Street
Indianapolis, IN 46240 USA

Reader Services

Visit our website and register this book at quepublishing.com/register for convenient access to any updates, downloads, or errata that might be available for this book.

Introduction

There's no question that social media is becoming big business. A report released by BAI Kinsley, a media consultancy, predicts that social media advertising spending will hit $9.8 billion by 2016, which represents a compounding annual growth rate of 21%.[1] According to the same report, spending in 2011 was $3.8 billion. To put the forecast in perspective, the IAB estimated that TV ad spending totaled $68.7 billion in 2010, while newspapers and radio took in $22.8 billion and $15.3 billion, respectively.[2] Those numbers don't include other types of social media spending like social media marketing, gaming, or social commerce. Marketers have been working hard to figure out where social media fits within their organizations and have been met with varying degrees of buy-in from their management teams. Although many executives are starting to come around to the idea that social media will be an important factor in driving their businesses, there still is a reasonable level of scrutiny. A 2011 study of C-level executives and vice presidents who were the primary decision makers on social media spending "found that only 27% listed social business as a top strategic

1. BIA Kelsey Social Media Press Release http://www.biakelsey.com/Company/Press-Releases/120515-U.S.-Social-Media-Ad-Spending-to-Reach-%249.8-Billion-by-2016.asp
2. Mashable http://mashable.com/2011/05/03/social-media-ad-spending-8b/

priority. Nearly half (47%) admitted a social plan was necessary but not a strategic priority, and 19% said social business strategy was simply not necessary."[3]

This is a drastic divergence from an earlier report released by Social Media Examiner that looked at marketers' perspectives on social media. In that report, 90% of marketers stated social media is important to their businesses.[4]

So, why is there such a large gap between the priorities of executives and those of marketers? The answer likely is a combination of differing priorities, differing perspectives on what drives business, and differing measurements of success. Marketers have been encouraged by growing followings and fan bases and by increasing engagement on social networks. Although this also encourages executives, it doesn't answer the big question on their minds, "What is the return on investment (ROI)?" This, unfortunately, is a big question that isn't as easy to answer as executives think it should be. The reality of social media measurement is that it can be really complicated. Just think about it for a second and ask yourself these questions:

- What report can I pull to tell me how much revenue was generated from (insert social media network)?
- Which report should I look at to know which status update had the highest conversion rate for prospective clients?
- Where can I find the data to show me how long a social media customer stays a customer?
- Do social media clients spend more or less than those who come through other marketing channels?
- Do social media clients buy more often than those who come through other marketing channels?
- Do prospects who come through the social media channel convert better or worse than those who come through other marketing channels?

These are tough questions. Unfortunately, the data that marketers need to answer these questions isn't readily available. Although many social media software vendors claim to measure ROI, the truth is there isn't a shiny social media measurement box that gives marketers all the insights their management team and executive team want. Thus, marketers haven't been able to make a strong enough case to compete for aggressive investment in the social channel. As a result, many executives are finding themselves in a state of cautious optimism when considering allocations toward social media initiatives. Marketing Sherpa's 2011 benchmark

---

3. 2011 Jive Social Business Index Survey

4. 2011 Social Media Marketing Industry Report released by Social Media Examiner

survey reported that 64% of executive-level respondents said, "Social marketing is a promising tactic that will eventually produce ROI. Let's invest, but do it conservatively."[5] This has become a chicken-or-the-egg scenario. Executives want the data. Marketers want to collect the data. Collecting the data may require costly technology platform integrations, and because executives are investing conservatively, marketers can't get to the numbers.

Redefining ROI

The result has been a lot of creativity around the term *ROI*. Great marketers are creative people. When faced with the challenge of not being able to measure ROI, the inclination is to ask, "What is ROI, really?" People are writing a flood of articles about ROI and how it relates to social media. First, they debate whether ROI *should* be measured. Questions like, "Do you measure the ROI of your phone, email, or how about your pants?" are laughable. But isn't the idea of measuring the ROI of social media laughable as well? The idea of going to executive teams and asking those questions is appealing. However, such a strategy wouldn't win you any brownie points and could even backfire so badly as to derail your efforts.

When snarky doesn't work, you might ask yourself, "What if I could *spin* ROI?" That's your job, right? To protect the company's reputation and make the brand look awesome, even in the direst circumstances. What if you applied this same creativity to ROI? Could you actually reframe the conversation around ROI to include something you might actually be able to measure? Several marketers tried, with varying levels of success. Interesting metrics like return on influence, return on conversation, and return on engagement entered the mix. Each provided a framework for a measurement that was deemed to provide a more comprehensive picture of social media's value than the boring, stark financial picture that traditional ROI would tell.

Return on influence is the measure of how a company's "influence" delivers a positive return to the company. Most articles about return on influence talk of it as a qualitative measure of return to a company. And there isn't a standard formula used for the calculation. You'll recognize the type of information you get from qualitative research if you've ever conducted a focus group or survey with open-ended questions. By its nature, qualitative data requires interpretation to derive the final answer, which is subjective. Subjective data can be considered less reliable because, after all, it's based on how you interpreted the responses. The concept is that if a company increases its influence, it will achieve a higher return. This concept is interesting, but the struggle is that social media is already fairly subjective.

---

5. 2011 Benchmark Survey Marketing Sherpa

If you add another subjective measure of success, you are probably going to raise some eyebrows with your management team. ROI is hard enough to measure, but return on influence is making data collection even more difficult and adds a manual process of data collection and analysis. Social media tools like Klout attempt to quantify influence to make this easier; however, there has been debate over whether their results are truly identifying influencers. Another tool called GroupHigh allows marketers to do a variety of searches to find blogger influencers and apply both quantitative data and subjective research to determine who the influencers are for a brand. Truly measuring influence requires quantitative data combined with a human touch, which makes scaling data collection more difficult.

Return on conversation is the measure of how participating in the conversation around your brand, products, and competition delivers a return to the company. This is another one that lacks a standard formula for measuring the results; however, it seems reasonable for a company to want to understand whether the time invested in social media monitoring and engagement is delivering value. The big question comes in when trying to determine how to define value.

Return on engagement measures the value that driving engagement from social media users brings to the company. In this context, engagement is quantifying the value of those who take a physical action to interact with your brand on a social media channel. For example, someone who retweets a message has engaged with your company. Out of the three returns, this is one that has quantifiable data that can be used for the calculation because any form of engagement on a social channel could be measured against the investment. Although this metric is certainly another derivative of ROI, it is one that may hold more weight in a board room than return on conversation.

There is a lot to be said for being creative and trying to figure out how to demonstrate social media value when the tough questions are asked. However, *creativity requires explanation.* Management teams are going to ask a lot of questions about what these metrics mean and how they demonstrate an impact on the bottom line. Quite frankly, there are enough problems with these questions when you try to explain the social media metrics you already have. When trying to explain what retweets, shares, fans, and followers are to your management team, you are fielding the same questions about their value and trying to find measures to explain why they matter.

Why Is This So Hard?

It's mindboggling that so many people think social media is immeasurable, when online marketing is one of the most measurable forms of marketing. You can track almost every action a person takes online. It is far more difficult to track actions taken after reading a newspaper article or seeing a particular billboard or TV ad. But for some reason, society has decided that social media is so important that it's necessary to create a whole set of metrics to explain it. Not so. This book will demonstrate how to use existing core metrics that are already well understood to show social media ROI so you don't have to start from scratch. One common argument is that existing metrics don't show the *value* of social media. It is fair to say that the full impact of social media may not be illustrated with existing metrics, and it is going to be a long time before there is enough data to show the full value social media brings to the table. But if you wait for the perfect data set, you are likely to lose management support for social media efforts unnecessarily. You can use the data you have at your fingertips today to show a positive return while you build the case for more holistic measures.

You've likely heard that there aren't industry standards for measuring social media. Not true. There *are* standard metrics for every area that social media touches, but they've been ignored in favor of something that doesn't quite exist yet. If marketers wait for standard social media measures and metrics to tell the whole story, someday they will try the patience of executives who are interested in social media ROI today. In a poll of 175 CMOs, BazaarVoice reported that 74% of them anticipated they would finally be able to tie social media to hard ROI in 2011. The reality is that the majority of those CMOs didn't get to ROI in 2011, which puts even more pressure on getting there now. Marketing Sherpa's 2011 Social Media Benchmark report revealed that a mere 20% of CMOs said that social marketing is producing a measurable ROI for their organization.[6] This means marketers need to find a way to answer these questions now, and you are going to have to accept the limitations that come with using financial metrics to demonstrate social media value.

Marketing teams have become so wrapped up in trying to demonstrate the full impact of social media that it has created a blind spot for itself. People blame the lack of a standardized measure for success for an inability to translate social media's contribution to the bottom line. They try to teach executives to understand the language of social media instead of translating social media into what matters to them. In the battle to measure social media value, people have diluted the conversation into a language that management teams don't understand. They've tried to create a new system of measurement to demonstrate value. They've spent time trying to explain why an increase in the number of mentions or the number of fans matters. Instead, the goal should be to keep it simple and focus on core business objectives that executives can relate to and understand.

---

6. 2011 Benchmark Survey Marketing Sherpa

What Management Teams Care About: Sales, Revenue, and Cost

Executives want to understand how social media contributes to the bottom line. And the bottom line is measured in terms of financial impact on sales volume, revenue, and cost. Management teams want you to translate social media impact into a language they understand and to realize they aren't going to take the time to care about why a retweet matters. It's important that you create a measurement framework that doesn't require a Ph.D. in Cool to understand. Management teams are getting tough questions about social media. And it's your job to give them data to make the case for continued investment in the marketing channel you've come to love. You can get these metrics today, and it isn't as hard as it's made out to be.

Ask to see a copy of your daily management team report. This report shows the metrics that are mission critical for your executives. They are the metrics they use to determine the health of the company, the progress toward organizational goals, and where they stand on profitability. They look at it every day! If you can show how social media affects any of those metrics, you will have no problem getting buy-in.

Common Metrics Found on Executive Reports		
YTD Revenue	MTD Revenue	% of MTD Revenue Goal Achieved
YTD Sales Volume	MTD Sales Volume	% of YTD Sales Goal Achieved
YTD COGS	MTD COGS	% of COGS Above or Below Goal
Cost Per Lead	Cost Per Sale	% Above or Below goal
Cost Per Call	Cost Per Click (Online)	Cost Per Impression
Lead Conversion Rate	Average Time to Close	Average Sales Receipt

YTD = Year to Date, MTD = Month to Date, COGS = Cost of Goods Sold

So why hasn't anyone figured out how to tie social media impact to these numbers? Is it possible? Absolutely. This book shows you how.

You know how important measurement is to demonstrate success. Social Media Examiner's 2012 Industry Report found that 40% of all social media marketers want to know how to monitor and measure their ROI.[7] The pump is primed, and you're ready to measure.

---

7.   2012 Social Media Marketing Industry Report released by Social Media Examiner

The question is, "How do you actually do it?" This book isn't a theoretical framework of social media measurement. Rather, it will give you a tested and proven framework for social media measurement that will win with your management team and help you rise to the top. Then it will show you what to measure, exactly how to measure it, and provide hands-on exercises so you will walk away with an actionable plan for turning your social media channel into a quantifiable contributor to the bottom line. This book is about action. So, prepare to act.

Hands-On Exercise: Getting Started

If you want to measure social media ROI, you'll need to get your hands dirty so you can figure out what metrics are important to your business. Most likely, you will see that the metrics you've been presenting to show social media's success don't correlate to the metrics that are used to drive business decisions. Don't worry. You aren't alone. The rest of the chapters will show you how to get your measurement reports in-line with what executives care about.

Activity 1: Get Your Hands Dirty

The first thing you need to do is get your hands on the daily executive report. Go to your manager and ask to get a copy of the daily report that the chief executive officer, chief financial officer, and chief marketing officer receive. If your manager asks why, say that you want to tie social media into the numbers that are important to them and you'd like to understand the benchmark they use for success. This will pique some interest—who could possibly object to that? By asking, you may have just made your manager your first internal champion. If you do meet resistance, ask for a list of the metrics on the report and the target goal for cost metrics—that is, cost per lead.

Hands-On Exercise: Activity 2: Get a Dose of Reality

The second step is to look at the reports you've been presenting to your management team to see how they stack up to the executive report. Don't worry if you can't answer "Yes" to any of these questions yet. This exercise is a review of where you are starting so that when you create your new framework for reporting, you can evaluate your success.

Question	Answer	Notes
Does your current report have any of the metrics that are on your executive report?	☐ Yes ☐ No	
Does your current report demonstrate how social media affected sales volume, revenue, and costs?	☐ Yes ☐ No	
Does your current report illustrate which social media activities are delivering the highest return?	☐ Yes ☐ No	
Does your current report help you make better decisions about which activities to increase?	☐ Yes ☐ No	
Does your current report help you make decisions about what activities to stop?	☐ Yes ☐ No	

If you answered "No" to any of these questions, it's time to align social media measurement to the metrics that will help you make better business decisions and demonstrate how social media is affecting the bottom line. A measurement framework that can help you adjust your social media strategy and tactics based on what is working will help you optimize your efforts and deliver a higher ROI. Additionally, a measurement framework that demonstrates how social media is moving the needle on core business objectives will give your management team the fuel it needs to justify your social media efforts to naysayers.

Aligning Social Media with Core Business Objectives

1

Aligning Social Media Strategies to Business Goals

For social media to deliver on core business objectives, you first need to decide which business goals you are trying to accomplish. When you do that, you'll have a list of core metrics you can use to evaluate success. A lot of companies started social media by setting up accounts on Twitter and Facebook and waiting to see what happened. They started listening to the conversation about their brand, their competitors, and their industry on social media networks. They set up a fan page to see who would like it and engage in conversation. They tried different types of content to see what would interest the audience. They relied on the theory of, "If we build it, they will come."

Did others come? Did audiences flock to engage with the brand?

Although some consumer brands found their names strong enough to drive audience engagement, far more struggled to build a following and wound up in a one-way conversation with a disengaged audience. Others saw their accounts become battlegrounds for disgruntled customers who took to social networks to share their displeasure. And even more found themselves listening to crickets. They were swayed to "listen" to the conversation because, after all, people are talking about the brand, and it's their choice whether to be a part of the conversation. For many, that was true. But for far more, it seemed no one was talking. This raised questions for brands about whether they should engage. After all, if no one is talking about the brand, clearly it's not necessary to be there, right? That really depends on what you are trying to accomplish.

Setting Social Media Goals

Every great strategy starts with a goal. Understand your purpose for engaging in social media. Further, understand your purpose for each social media account. If you are on Facebook or Twitter and you don't know what you are trying to accomplish, how it will advance your mission, whether you are reaching your target audience, or how you will provide value to your followers, you probably shouldn't be on Twitter or Facebook. Social media has moved beyond the "try it and see" approach; it's time to get strategic about your presence.

Getting strategic about your social media approach, so you can measure your results, starts with defining your goals (see Figure 1.1). Marketing has three primary goals: increasing brand awareness, generating leads, and retaining your existing customers. Brand awareness is aimed at generating more exposure and getting more eyeballs on your brand. The goal is to have more people who recognize your brand and know your company's name. Lead generation is about finding more sales and revenue opportunities for your company. It's about using marketing to sell more products or services. Customer retention is about keeping your existing customers coming back for more.

You can use social media effectively to accomplish all three of these goals. However, it is difficult to do all three at once unless you have an extremely large marketing budget and extensive resources.

Marketing teams that are trying to do everything at once with social media wind up with mediocrity. You can't be great at everything when you are keeping so many balls in the air. Not to mention that many marketers who are responsible for social media had that responsibility added on to their "real jobs." They're trying to fit the management of those 20 new social media initiatives into their already full-time jobs. Overwhelmed marketers who want to see a light at the end of this extremely busy tunnel start to ask, "What can I take away if social media starts working?" "Can I replace direct mail with social media?" "Can I replace advertising with social media?" "Can I replace PR with social media?"

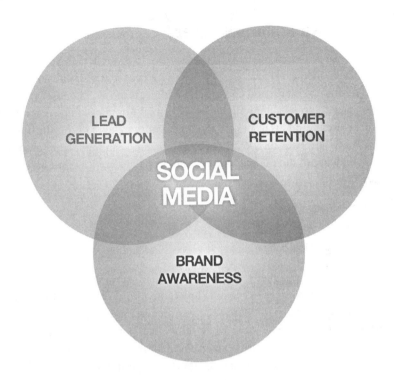

Figure 1.1   *Social media helps to achieve three common marketing goals.*

This book doesn't make a case for social media to replace other marketing channels. Social media is not a silver bullet that will solve your marketing problems. Instead, this book is about maximizing the efficiency of the time you spend on social media to deliver the best return. This book is about showing you how social media complements other marketing channels and about recognizing that social media does not and should not be placed in a silo. Social media can only be successful if you integrate and support it through other marketing channels. When you do this, social media raises the success levels of all marketing efforts and increases your ability to measure and demonstrate that success.

But first, you need to figure out where social media is best positioned to generate success. If you are trying to do everything, you probably are doing it all halfway, which will limit your success. So rather than having that unrealistic list of 20 social media initiatives aimed at achieving all three goals, it is best to pick one goal and be awesome at it. If you are able to effectively move the needle with one goal, it will be much easier to justify asking for the resources to start another initiative.

Goal 1: Increase Brand Awareness

A common goal for social media is to increase brand awareness in your target audience. Social media enables you to reach more people at a significantly lower cost than traditional marketing channels; therefore, it should increase brand awareness and brand recall among buyers who might not have known about your company before. Brand awareness is about getting more eyeballs on the brand, and marketers have been working to attract attention and keep brands top of mind for decades. Think about the notable advertising campaigns you've come across during the Super Bowl:

- Budweiser's Clydesdales
- Go Daddy's hot women
- E-Trade's talking baby

These campaigns are designed to do one thing: be memorable. Brands are also using innovative approaches like product placement to capture the attention of those who skip through commercials. There are blatant examples of product placement in the TV show *30 Rock* while shows like *The Office* do a great job of integrating products into the story line. Although there are new creative approaches to generate brand awareness, companies are also still using more traditional tactics like sponsorships and trade shows to get in front of a new captive audience. That's what brand awareness is all about. In social media, you look at how you can develop relationships and provide value to your target audience, which will help you remain top of mind when the audience makes a buying decision.

There have been some great examples of social media in both the business-to-consumer (B2C) and business-to-business (B2B) marketing spaces. It would be easy to show you examples from huge consumer brands that have multi-billion dollar budgets. Instead, let's look at a different kind of B2C success story.

King Arthur Flour Generates Brand Awareness and Loyalty with Social Media

Flour? It's impossible to get people to care about flour, right? Wrong. King Arthur Flour took an interesting approach to social media. Rather than focusing on the benefits of using its flour, it focuses on the end product—the food its product helps to create. King Flour has created a corporate blog where it shares recipes for delicious food, a Twitter account where it talks to cooks and bakers about the great food they create, and a Facebook account where it shares fantastic photos of food, recipes, and tips. As a result, King Arthur Flour has captured an audience of more than 63,000 Facebook fans and more than 13,000 followers on Twitter. The content the company posts generates a reasonable number of replies, showing that its audience is engaged (see Figure 1.2). This unlikely consumer brand has generated substantial brand awareness by using social media.

Figure 1.2   *King Arthur Flour uses cooking tips to increase awareness.*

Radian6 Has Become a Go-To Resource for Marketers Through Social Media Efforts

It's always interesting to hear the perspective that social media only works for consumer brands because it has succeeded in the B2B marketing space. The key issue is whether your target audience is paying attention to what you have to say. For example, Radian6 has been able to effectively target marketers on Twitter with compelling content that helps them do their jobs with a better understanding of the social media landscape. This content is clearly branded with the Radian6 logo, and online marketers have come to respect its content and refer to it as best-in-breed. This brand recognition helps to ensure that when marketers need a social media monitoring solution, they will think of Radian6. The brand recognition Radian6 achieved caught the attention of Salesforce, a leading customer relationship management (CRM) software provider, and it snapped up the company for an estimated $326 million in March 2011.

It's easy to think of brand awareness as an easy win for social media, and most companies are trying to accomplish some level of brand awareness through the social channel, even if their primary goal is something else. But remember those crickets from earlier? Brand awareness can be difficult. It requires a substantial effort toward building an engaged audience that is willing to consistently share your content with their networks. Growing an audience takes time, and although brand awareness is one of the easier social media goals to measure, it is one of the harder goals to accomplish because it requires time, content, and that brands be interesting.

Goal 2: Generate More Leads

Most companies want to have more business coming through the door. Social media can effectively generate more leads for your business. A lead is someone who has expressed interest in your products and has provided contact information at some point in the sales process.

Depending on your business model, leads can also be called qualified applications, prospective donors, prospects, or potential clients. Whatever you call a lead, it is possible to effectively create and nurture leads for your company through social media channels. Your B2B sales team or B2C marketing campaign can target those leads for conversion. However, it is important to understand how the social media lead compares to other types of leads and how to effectively market to the lead to generate a sale. This will be covered in depth in Chapter 6, "Measuring Social Media for Lead Generation."

Openly discussing that your company is trying to generate more leads in social media may cause people to raise a few eyebrows. Why? Because companies have come onto Twitter or Facebook to try to sell their products and services to anyone who will listen. They have set up accounts and started screaming their offers at potential customers, while those customers run the other direction as quickly as possible. People walk away after an experience like that feeling like they need a shower. Why is that such a bad experience?

Overpromotion

Social media is built for a two-way conversation. Yet, there are glaring examples of companies who are using the channel to broadcast their promotions rather than build relationships and encourage dialogue. If you look at the Twitter account for eOne Home Video, a DVD service company, you will find tweet after tweet about its latest promotion. To attract attention to its status updates, it uses combinations of all caps and hashtags for celebrities who are in the videos it promotes.

This type of promotion is effective in advertising channels like Google Adwords. But, in social media, it comes across as tacky. Would you follow this Twitter account? Perhaps if you were a DVD lover you might, but many would look at this and recognize that while it informs you of the latest promotion, it won't add value to your movie-watching experience. A more engaging approach might be to provide interesting tidbits about the actors in the movies eOne is promoting. eOne could also ask for opinions from those who have already seen the movie. Questions like, "What was your favorite episode of *Hell on Wheels*?" would elicit conversation around the release that ties back to eOne.

Shameless Selling Doesn't Work—Making It Easy to Buy Does

The reason you likely have such a bad taste in your mouth about making money from social media is that so many companies have taken to social networks and handled it like eOne. They have turned their social media networks into a broadcast platform for special promotions rather than an engaging dialogue. This is what happens when marketers treat social media like every other marketing channel that is designed to "get your offer out."

A more effective lead-generation strategy for social media is making it *super easy to buy when the client is ready to buy*. Think about your favorite fan pages, and then think about what you would have to do to purchase something from that company. Would you have to click on the Info tab, find the company's website, go to the site, and search for how to buy? Too often this is the exact experience people have on a business fan page. And it's too much for most lazy consumers. If you don't make it easy, people will put buying down as something to do later and probably forget.

Effective lead-generation strategies also recognize the difference between a social media lead and leads that come through other marketing channels and build marketing campaigns to nurture the sales. (This will be covered in Chapter 5, "Social Media for Lead Generation.") If you do your job well, the relationships you build in social media will result in sales. And you can design your social media content to facilitate your sales process, overcome objections, and build relationships with clients before your competition even knows the clients exist. It is about "being there before the sale" as Greg Cangialosi, former CEO of Blue Sky Factory, is known to say.

As you become active on social media networks, you will develop relationships with people you may never have met otherwise. At some point, they may purchase your products. If you aren't measuring the number of sales that result from the relationships forged on those networks, social media may be getting short-changed in your company. Lead generation in social media is becoming a reality as marketers come to terms with the fact that they are going to have to show a positive return from social media. There is a large movement toward inbound lead generation—toward building activities that will draw potential clients, toward building platforms to create databases full of website visitors that catalog their interests. Instead of going out to find qualified leads, instead of chasing down possible leads, companies are using social media to bring those potential clients to them.

HubSpot Offers a Shining Example of Effective Lead-Generation Strategies

The best example comes from the inbound lead-generation company, HubSpot. HubSpot has taken content marketing to a different level. It is a B2B software company that focuses on providing the resources marketers need to understand inbound marketing and lead-generation efforts from the online channel. On its blog, HubSpot provides tips and resources. It produces e-books and webinars for marketers to get more in-depth information. It uses Twitter to host chats, share resources, and answer marketers' questions about generating leads online. On Facebook, HubSpot shares social media industry news and interesting data. On Google+, HubSpot focuses on promoting its resources and highlighting industry events its team members will attend. The content HubSpot produces is extremely relevant to its audience, and it has earned the right to talk about itself by providing a tremendous amount of value to marketers. Of course, HubSpot's secret sauce is collecting contact information from marketers who download its resources, and putting leads into the sales funnel (see Figure 1.3). Its software is designed to develop landing pages that convert viewers to customers, and it practices what it preaches. This book discusses more about what HubSpot does in Chapter 5.

Under Armour Makes It Super Easy to Buy

In the B2C world, Under Armour is a fantastic example of how a company makes it easy for fans and followers to buy. It uses Twitter to follow conversations around sports, congratulate teams on wins, and respond to feedback about its products. And on Facebook, Under Armour really shines. It provides tips for athletes, takes polls on what athletes find important, and shares interviews with celebrity users of Under Armour products. It engages its following in conversations and encourages them to share opinions. Under Armour doesn't stop at asking how training is going for its fans; it asks pointed questions about what fans consider when making a purchase decision for products it carries. Then it makes those products easy to buy. Under Armour built a Facebook app dedicated to selling its products. You can shop for any of its products, watch videos about the products, and if you see a photo with a product you want, you can click on the image to see what the product is and immediately make a purchase (see Figures 1.4, 1.5, and 1.6).

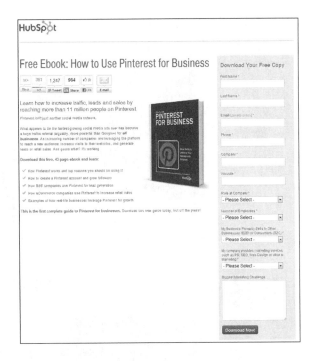

Figure 1.3   *HubSpot uses valuable content with lead forms to convert social media leads.*

Figure 1.4   *Under Armour has an online store within Facebook.*

Figure 1.5   *The Under Armour online store provides an engaging user experience.*

Figure 1.6   *Clicking a plus sign displays the product with a "BUY NOW" button.*

Retaining Your Existing Customers

Another common goal for social media is to keep your existing customers happy and coming back for more. Companies invest large amounts of money to bring new clients in the door. If you can keep them as return customers, their value to the company continues to rise.

You've seen the rise of social media accounts dedicated to serving customers, including Boingo, Best Buy's Twelpforce, and Comcast. These accounts answer customer questions in real time and escalate complaints to the appropriate channels. It is a great option for customers who prefer to reach a service representative online without having to call and wait on hold forever.

How Do I Know Which Goal Is Right for My Company?

How do you know which goal to select? How do you know which goal will be able to deliver? How do you know which goal will drive the company's mission forward? Is there a right or a wrong answer?

Under Armour understands that consumers are busy. It also understands that those busy customers are spending valuable time on Facebook, and thus they need to be able to purchase Under Armour products while they're there. This is smart marketing; it clears away any barriers to making a purchase. Companies should make it easy for customers to buy the products they're interested in, wherever they happen to interact with them.

Both of these are great examples of using social media to generate more leads and more revenue. Most companies are looking to increase revenues, so if you can tie your social media efforts to lead generation, it is much easier to get buy-in from your management team. However, that comes with caution because lead generation in social media is an art form that must be handled with finesse.

Goal 3: Increasing Customer Retention

The third goal of marketing is to keep existing customers happy. This does two things: It provides better customer service to those customers, and it increases revenues through those customers' repeat business. But you can be more strategic about increasing those revenues.

You've probably heard the mantra, "It's cheaper to keep your existing customers than it is to get new ones" at least a hundred times. There is a lot of truth in that little statement. It's amazing how marketers will work so hard to get customers and then turn them over to the customer service team and forget about them. Your existing customer database is a gold mine for increasing revenue, if you know how to keep them happy and coming back for more. Social media is an excellent channel for two-way communication with your existing customer base. You can use it to answer questions, respond to feedback, and share client success stories. The beauty of the two-way conversation is that you can elicit customer feedback on product ideas and get an immediate response before spending a lot of money to develop products your customers don't want or need.

Social media can help marketers start to understand what their customers' needs, wants, and desires are, instead of trying to get inside their heads and guess. The reality is that marketers are not their customers. The two-way conversation that is created in social media can help you understand the voice of your customer and user behavior. This insight can be used to help improve your products and services, create new products to solve customer problems, and improve internal processes to provide better services. By better understanding customers, marketers can deliver better results in all aspects of their jobs.

Using Social Media for Customer Service

Several brands have excelled at providing awesome customer service through social media. When customers are asking questions about your brand or product, you want to make sure you are participating in that conversation. If you aren't, either the question will go unanswered—which can make your company look unresponsive—or, even worse, someone else could answer incorrectly. If you have customers who are actively using social media to talk about your products or services, you need to consider how you can engage them.

Some brands use social media for customer service to provide tips and resources and answer questions. Some also effectively manage customer complaints, using the feedback to improve customer service issues that weren't being handled otherwise.

Boingo Wireless Manages Customer Service on Twitter and Facebook

The Wi-Fi hotspot provider Boingo uses Twitter and Facebook almost exclusively to answer customer questions. It helps customers get online through its Wi-Fi network almost anywhere in the world. When customers have issues getting online, many take to their social network of choice on their mobile devices. And they complain. Boingo offers several hotspots in airports, which means getting customers online quickly and efficiently is important to keeping its customers happy. And if customers do complain, Boingo is right there to help them get online quickly and efficiently, with a smile (see Figure 1.7).

Figure 1.7 *Boingo uses Twitter and Facebook to help clients get online.*

Infusionsoft Becomes a Business Adviser

Infusionsoft has taken a different approach to providing a great customer experience on its social networks. It answers a customer's question on Twitter, Facebook, or Google+, but its reason for being there is different. Infusionsoft is a customer relationship management system (CRM) and marketing automation tool designed for small businesses. It serves a huge market of small businesses that might have 1–20 employees, be stretched for time and resources, and be struggling to market themselves. Infusionsoft's niche is marketing automation. Therefore, Infusionsoft provides resources, guides, webinars, and other types of content designed to help its clients better market their products and services (see Figure 1.8).

Figure 1.8   *Infusionsoft teaches clients how to be better marketers.*

In essence, Infusionsoft has become an outsourced chief marketing officer for its clients, providing them with everything they need to know to build a strong marketing plan and use their tool to help execute it. Its business model is built on a monthly fee based on the number of users. If its small businesses grow, it will need more software licenses for their new employees, which will increase revenues for Infusionsoft. Infusionsoft provides valuable information for its customers on its website, but it recognizes that some customers might not realize all this information is available. Therefore, it uses social media to drive customers to its latest content and answers customer questions.

Selecting the Right Social Media Goal

On to the big question: "Which goal is right for your company?" Any of the three goals could be good choices; however, it is important to evaluate goals based on how well they align with your resource limitations, how your strategies show notable progress toward the goal, and how important the goal is for the company. There isn't a right or a wrong answer. But there are choices that will enable you to get and keep buy-in from your management team.

Once you know what you are trying to achieve with your social media efforts, the metrics to measure your progress become clear. But selecting that goal can be tricky. Every company could select any of the three goals of brand awareness, lead generation, or customer retention and see success through the social channel, so there isn't technically a wrong answer. But the idea is to pick the goal that will get you buy-in quickly so the question of whether social media is worth the investment will fade away. There are a few things to consider before choosing the goal that is most appropriate.

Show Early Success

A primary objective for your company might be to increase revenues, so you might jump first to the goal for increasing leads. However, if your company has a standard sales cycle of 24 months, it will be difficult to keep your management team engaged and excited about what social media is delivering; the leads you are generating might have a longer sales cycle than standard leads. It is important to select an initial goal that will generate early success, which, in turn, will fuel support for expansion of your efforts to target another goal. You need to sell management on your ideas by using the goal that works the fastest. That doesn't mean that you don't lay the ground work for another goal at the same time; down the line you will reap the rewards from both.

Align the Social Media Goal with Business Goals

Make sure you understand what your company's big goals are for the next 12–24 months. Which business drivers are your executive team focused on? That's where the secret for your success will come from. The business plan provides a map of what is important to your management team; use it to find something that you can use social media to help them achieve.

Say you tell the management team that your goal with social media is to provide customer service online. If the business plan is aimed at doubling revenues in two years, you would get the "Okay, go do that feel-good stuff" brush off. Now, what if, knowing the goal is more revenue, you instead said, "Our goal with social media is to increase revenue with our existing customers. We are going to make sure they are satisfied, get them to spend more money at each transaction, buy more often, and refer more business our way." You would get a very different response. You haven't changed your goal for social media, but you have shown the management team how social media is going to affect what is important to them: the doubled revenues.

Make Sure You Can Measure Success

Companies have an array of systems in place and varying abilities to measure their results. It's important that you select a goal that your company is positioned to measure. You will need to show whether you are moving the needle toward your goal, and if your company can't measure it, you will have a tough time showing results.

One of the most difficult areas of measurement for social media is impact on revenue. It requires you to be able to connect a response to a tweet to how much a prospect or customer has spent. To measure impact on revenue, there needs to be a conversation between the social channel and your CRM system where sales are monitored. We'll go through this in depth in Chapter 9, "Breaking Down the Barriers to Social Media Measurement," and show you how to navigate these barriers, but for now you'll need to do a gut check to gauge the likelihood of being able to make that connection. If your company hasn't been able to measure how any marketing campaign has contributed to revenue, it is far less likely you'll be able to do it for social media. It's possible, of course, but it is more of an uphill battle. If your company can't tell which marketing campaigns are most effective at retaining customers, it will be equally difficult to measure an increase in revenue from existing customers. Again, this doesn't make the goals impossible to achieve; it just makes them more difficult to measure in terms of sales volume and revenues. Here are a few questions you can ask yourself to see which goal might be the best to show early success.

Brand Awareness Questions	Yes	No
Can we capitalize on an already well-known brand name?		
Do we have resources to dedicate to creating compelling content designed for our target market?		
Are there organizations with larger audiences that we could partner with to do joint content marketing promotions?		
Do we have an advertising budget that could help support content distribution?		

If the answer to these questions is "Yes," brand awareness may be a good choice. Remember, we want to show early success, and building brand awareness is an activity that takes time. Fortunately, when you work to achieve both lead generation and customer retention, the side benefit is an increase in brand awareness. But you wouldn't want to hinge your success on an increase in awareness because it might take longer than showing the success with the other two goals. Even with the example of Radian6 from earlier, it is clear that the primary goal is to use content to drive more inbound leads. Radian6 was able to do this effectively through resources that were shared from marketer to marketer, and this led to a dramatic increase in brand awareness at the same time. But Radian6 didn't go to market in social media measuring its success on increasing awareness. It still measures its results in terms of the number of quality inbound leads.

If you have the resources to create great content and either have a great brand following now, or can look to partner with organizations who do, you will have better success in showing results with brand awareness metrics. If you answered no to the previous questions, ask yourself the following questions:

Customer Retention Questions	Yes	No
Can I find my existing customers on social media sites?		
Do my customers have conversations about my brand on social media networks that I am not participating in?		
Is there an opportunity to use social media to connect with existing customers and build a stronger one-on-one relationship with them?		

If you answered "Yes" to these questions, customer retention may be a good choice. When considering a social media strategy for customer retention, the first question becomes, "Are my existing customers using social media?" And if so, "How?" Then, "Which social media channels are they using?" If your customers are actively using social networks and talking about your company, whether they are saying good or bad things, you have a responsibility to engage them, answer their questions, and fix customer service issues. Unfortunately, when people are happy they tend not to say anything. But when people are unhappy, they tend to share their displeasure with their networks. If you don't respond to their complaints and show that you are trying to resolve their problems, future clients might see these unaddressed negative posts. That can shape the way your brand is perceived in the marketplace. However, if you respond and show that you are attempting to fix the issue, potential clients will see that and be more likely to believe that you will help them if they are unhappy.

Tip

> Go to http://topsy.com and search for your brand name. It will give you an idea of how much conversation is happening on Twitter about your brand. Use http://kurrently.com to search both Facebook and Twitter at the same time. Remember, you will only see posts on Facebook that have been shared publicly. Then go to Google+ and use the search bar to search for your brand name. Make sure you have selected "google+ posts, from everyone, for everyone" in the bar under the search box. Finally, go to http://google.com and search for your brand name; then click on Blogs in the left column. This returns all the blogs that have mentioned your brand name. Click on Everything in the left column, and do a search for your brand with the word *reviews*—that is, *HubSpot reviews*. This will return all the results that have reviews of your company.

If your customers talk about your company on social media sites, you should participate in the conversation. The beauty of this scenario is that you can show your management team what is being said. You can show the negativity and ask, "Do we want people to believe this?" You can show the positivity and ask, "Shouldn't we say thank you?" When the conversation is there, it is easy to get the fuel you need to get the management team behind you. If you answered "No" to the preceding questions, customer retention might not be a good fit for your organization. Try these questions to see whether lead generation will be a better option.

Lead Generation Questions	Yes	No
Does my company have online lead-generation forms that can be leveraged for high-value social media content like e-books and webinars? If not, does the company have the resources to create them?		
Does the company have a library of content that can be used or repurposed to track interest in products and services? If not, does the company have the resources to create some?		
Does the company have a relatively short sales cycle that will allow leads to convert and close this year (that is, less than six months for a typical sale)?		
Does the team who will be responsible for social media understand that a pushy, buy-now sales approach won't work, and that their job is to build relationships, not to force the sale?		

If you can make it super easy to buy from the social channel by leveraging lead forms in exchange for high-value content, lead generation might be a good choice. If your sales cycle is shorter than six months, you should be able to show positive results early enough to focus on lead generation. Most importantly, your social media team has to understand how social media works and that they can't be out there pushing your products like a door-to-door sales person. If you meet these criteria, lead generation is a viable choice for your company.

So, what if you answered "No" to all of those questions? What if you don't have a well-known brand or customers talking about you on social media sites? What if you don't have a library of content or lead-generation forms? First, don't panic. It just means that showing success in social media is going to take a little longer. You are going to have to set expectations with your management team on how long it will take to show tangible results. The first year may be a building year, where you focus on putting the right pieces in place and "getting your house in order." To determine which part of the house to get in order, look at your company's business plan. Determine whether brand awareness, customer retention, or lead generation will have the biggest effect on the company's goals. (If your customers aren't on social media sites talking about you, there isn't much you can do there for customer retention.) Once you've selected between brand awareness, customer retention, and lead generation, start charting your path with the tips throughout this book. You can build a successful social media strategy, but your first step is going to be to lay the groundwork for success. It might mean you need to complete some changes to your website, or that you need to have some content developed. As you get through this book, it will become clear what you need to put in place to get your strategy in full swing.

With all of these goals, you'll notice that it isn't about whether your company wants to achieve them. It's about whether your audience is there, how the audience is interacting, and how quickly you will be able to show success. Social media isn't going to fix all your marketing problems overnight; it is certainly more about the marathon than the sprint. But you have to understand the mindset of your management team. The executive team members control the purse strings, and they are coming around to the idea that they need a social media presence. It is your job to show them why and what results they should expect. There are plenty of intangible benefits of developing a strong social media strategy, and you'll high-five your team members as your relationships and conversations with your customers grow. But when you talk to your management team, you'll show them how social media affects the bottom line.

Although brand awareness can be the end goal, it is also a very good supporting goal for lead generation and customer retention. If you do your job well in increasing leads or keeping your customers happy, brand awareness will result.

As you look at the three goals, rank them based on their ability to make an impact. You should walk away with a primary, secondary, and tertiary goal for social media before you move on to the next chapter, which focuses on understanding where social media and these goals fit into the sales funnel. If you want to understand how these goals affect the bottom line, you should probably make sure you understand the steps to get to the bottom line, right? You bet.

Hands-On Exercise: Selecting a Social Media Goal

The hardest part about selecting a goal for social media is knowing which one to select. All three of the core goals are viable options for most companies. This exercise will walk you through the necessary steps to help you determine which initial goal is best for your social media efforts.

Activity 1: Plot Existing Marketing Tactics

One exercise that can help you select a goal is to look at what your other marketing efforts are working to accomplish. Examine the three circles and place the marketing tactics you are already doing, either in the circle they align with, or between circles if they have more than one purpose (see Figure 1.9). Your goal at the end of this exercise is to select one goal as your primary goal for social media. Although all three goals may be viable options for your company, it is important to start with the goal that you can demonstrate the most success with first.

Do you see any of the goals that you don't have activities to achieve? If so, why don't you have anything working in that area? Is it because it isn't a priority for the company, or is it because you don't have the budget or resources to address it? If you see a goal that isn't getting much support, it might present a great opportunity for social media. On the flip side, if you see an area that has a lot of support, it can be equally as good a goal for social media. Typically, the goal that gets the most marketing support is one that is deemed very important for the company. So, it's worth considering whether social media can play a positive role there, too.

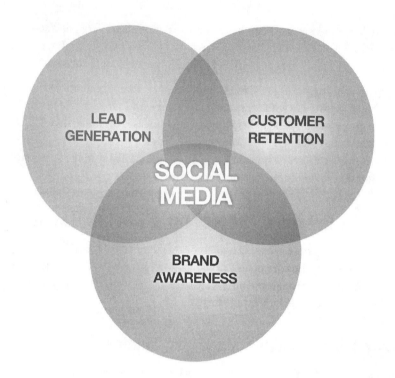

Figure 1.9 *Write your existing marketing activities on the goal they support to find opportunities for social media.*

Activity 2: SWOT Analysis

After you've looked at your marketing activities, look at your company's strengths, weaknesses, opportunities, and threats (SWOTs) with each of these goals.

In the following chart, write down your company's strengths and weaknesses for each of the three goals. For example, a strength might be that you have an existing infrastructure and solid plan for how the company wants to achieve lead generation, whereas a limitation might be that your sales cycle is 36 months, which might take too long to show success. Next to the strengths and weakness, write down any opportunities you have to overcome the limitations presented. An opportunity might be to focus on generating leads that can be turned over to the sales team at a lower cost than other channels. Finally, list any external threats that might hurt your ability to be successful. An external threat is a threat that you have no control over and might be happening outside of the company.

Goal	Strengths	Weaknesses	Opportunities	Threats

Which goal is rising to the top as the best opportunity for short-term success? Which goal is rising to the top as the best opportunity for long-term success? Which goal has too many barriers? Prioritize the three goals based on your findings.

2

Aligning Social Media to the Sales Funnel

Executives care about impact on sales volume, revenue, and cost. Management teams need to understand how social media is affecting the bottom line to give their full support. Why? Because they are held accountable for the company's bottom line. So, if you can show them how social media fits into their ability to achieve bottom line results, a light bulb goes off, and they start to get it. Everyone would love to walk into their management team and say, "So I want to try this new thing...it's, uh, called social media...I'm not sure what it is going to, like, deliver to, you know, the company...but my friends tell me it's, like, pretty awesome...so, like, can I have permission to go play on Facebook?" Business just doesn't work that way. Management teams aren't going to say it's okay to go play on Facebook when there is little chance of return. Remember, management teams weren't always managers; they started out just like you did, but through success and failure, good managers have learned that to be successful you have to understand what you are trying to achieve.

The best way to show them how social media contributes to the bottom line is to show them where it fits into the sales funnel. Have you ever noticed how many executives have a sales or finance background? Why do you think it's so common to have a board and executive team with so many people who started in sales and finance? They innately understand the sales funnel, they know how to grow revenue, and they have been able to demonstrate why an initiative is important to the bottom line. Most management teams live, eat, and breathe the sales funnel. It is a tool that has been used for decades to illustrate the sales and revenue-generation process. Now you're going to learn how to use the sales funnel to your advantage.

The traditional sales funnel starts when a prospective customer does something that triggers your sales process—scheduling a meeting with a salesperson or responding to a pay-per-click ad. From there, the stages a prospect goes through will vary based on the industry and the length of the sales cycle. What stays the same is that the traditional sales funnel starts when a prospect indicates an inclination to buy. But social media allows your company to "extend" its sales funnel (see Figure 2.1).

Figure 2.1   *Social media extends the sales funnel.*

Figure 2.1 illustrates five categories in the social media sales funnel. These define where a prospect is in the buying cycle and provide a clear list of metrics to measure activities within these stages. Further, these categories align with the three goals discussed in the first chapter. To get started, look at the top of the funnel.

Where Brand Awareness Fits

The first three categories of the new sales funnel align with the goals for brand awareness. *Exposure* is a measure of brand reach. *Influence* is a measure of how many influencers helped to spread the message. *Engagement* is a measure of how many people interacted with your brand. Each category brings the potential buyer closer to a potential sale.

Exposure

The exposure section of the sales funnel focuses on brand reach. The idea is that the more people who see your brand, the more people are likely to remember your brand. This is essentially the first stage in measuring brand awareness activities. Exposure doesn't only apply to social media; it also is a key goal in other marketing channels like public relations and advertising in TV, radio, and online. The top of the funnel is important because the more people you put into the top of the funnel, the more opportunities your company has to create sales.

Exposure is really about eyeballs. How many people have the potential to see a message from your brand? In public relations and online advertising, this is measured in impressions. You've likely seen reports that show how many impressions were generated as a result of public relations activities or banner and pay-per-click advertising.

You can use metrics that are widely accepted in public relations and online advertising to measure social media exposure, as well. In social media, fans, followers, and subscribers all have the potential to see your updates. Potential is an important element of exposure. Impressions in public relations are typically measured by the circulation, viewers, or listeners that each media outlet has. There is no guarantee that each person who receives a publication, watches a TV show, or listens to the radio station will actually hear or see your advertisement or media mention. But the potential is there. In online advertising, many rates are calculated on a cost-per-impression basis. Although this is transitioning to a cost-per-action and cost-per-lead model, most online outlets still provide reporting that shows the impressions for your advertising. Similar to PR, impressions don't equate to the number of people on the other end of the computer screen who actually notice your ad, but it has become a standard top-line measure of audience reach.

Your management team needs to understand that the more exposure you generate for the brand, the more opportunities the company will have to create sales. Social media provides an opportunity to significantly increase the number of people who are exposed to your brand at a fraction of the cost of public relations, TV, radio, and online advertising. Several core metrics are used to quantify exposure in social media. The table that follows gives some examples from a few social media channels.

Twitter	Facebook	YouTube	LinkedIn
Impressions from content	Total reach	Channel views	Displayed in search results

Influence

The next category in the new sales funnel is influence. The influence section describes those people who were exposed to your brand by an influencer in your industry. This is a separate category from exposure because those who are exposed to your brand by an influencer convert more like those who found out about your company through a referral from a friend. Influencers have loyal followers, fans, and readers who trust their opinions. Therefore, when they mention your brand, their words carry more credibility and influence than when you mention your brand yourself. That's why these people are one stage down in the sales funnel; they're more likely to buy than someone who might have seen one of your status updates.

Companies are starting to recognize the power of influence, and it has created a need to measure how influential people are. Companies like Klout have created algorithms to put a numerical value on people's influence. Although Klout's algorithm has faced a lot of skepticism, the reality is that influence is becoming a marketable business for those who have developed a strong following. And Klout is attempting to not only measure influence, but create a marketplace where you can search for influencers in topics that are relevant to your industry. It is an approach to social influence that recognizes that businesses need to start paying attention to those who are truly influential in their space.

Further, by having a category for influence in measurement, you can quantify the value companies achieve from strategies that focus on influencer outreach. To quantify that value, you measure how many influencers mention the brand, estimate the reach achieved through those efforts, and in the next category of the funnel measure the response the company received. Sample metrics are provided in the table that follows. Similar to exposure, you are still measuring those who had the potential to see the message, based on the influencer's reach.

Calculated from the Networks of Influencers Who Mention the Brand Only on the Networks on Which the Brand Was Mentioned					
Blog	Twitter	Facebook	Google+	YouTube	LinkedIn
RSS sub-scribers	Followers	Fans	Followers	Channel subscribers	Connections
Average monthly site traffic	Followers of those who retweet post	Friends of those who engage	Followers of those who +1	# of video embeds	# of group members
					# of questions voted as best answer

Engagement

The engagement category of the funnel is exactly what it sounds like. Here you can start to quantify those who are engaging with the brand in the social channel. This is a large category for social media, and it's where the value of social media starts to become clear to management teams when you quantify the results. There has been a lot of discussion and debate around engagement and what it means. But for these purposes, engagement means anyone who took a physical action during the time frame being measured to interact with your brand.

Think about all the opportunities someone has to engage with a brand on the variety of social networks available. Consider blogs, Twitter, and Facebook. Seriously, stop reading and think about the physical actions a person could take to engage in each of these.

Did you come up with a pretty robust list? That's because social media's big differentiator from traditional marketing channels is its ability to facilitate two-way interactions. There are many ways people can interact with the brand on social media sites because that is what social media was designed to do.

It's almost unfair to compare social media to traditional marketing channels based on engagement. How can you really interact with a newspaper article? Maybe you could hand someone else the article, but that is not measurable. PR firms have tried to capture this reach with what has been called a *pass-along multiplier*. But that's about as reliable as your grandma's rusty 1950 Buick Super would be for a cross-country trip. You could argue that pass-along multipliers were created to provide PR firms with a metric that could be used to make results look better. You'll find the same issue with TV and radio advertising; the only engagement is to actually respond to the advertisement. But if you aren't an interested buyer, you can't really "share" the offer with someone. And with online advertising you run into the same issue; other than responding to the ad yourself, it isn't shareable. Therefore, when you compare engagement across channels, social media perform exceptionally well.

Engagement is placed one level further into the sales funnel because the theory is that people are more likely to buy from your brand if they have taken the time to engage with it. You can assume that you will have higher brand recall from someone who engaged with your brand than from someone who was only exposed to the brand. Ben Franklin once wrote, "Tell me and I'll forget. Show me and I might remember. Involve me and I will understand." This held true in a study conducted by the Austin-based PulsePoint Group and The Economist Intelligence Unit. It showed that companies that embrace social engagement are experiencing up to four times greater business impact than less socially engaged rivals.[1] The following table gives you a list of metrics from a few of the core social networks that you can use as a guide. Remember, you'll want to calculate these metrics for a specific time period.

One question that comes up is, "What if someone is on my blog and she clicks to share a post on Twitter? Where is she counted?" You could argue to count her on either the originating channel or the channel where the information is shared. There isn't a right answer; you just want to make sure you calculate her in the same channel consistently so you aren't double-counting the numbers. For this illustration, we'll count the end destination. This makes pulling data a little cleaner for reporting.

There are a myriad of ways someone can engage with your brand on social networks. Unfortunately, the difference between the ways you can engage and the ease of getting the data to report on it varies greatly from channel to channel. You'll review this in depth later, and you'll get some tips to streamline data collection.

---

1. PulsePoint Group and The Economist Intelligence Unit

Blog	Twitter	Facebook	Google+	YouTube	LinkedIn
RSS subscribers	Followers	Fans	Followers	Subscribers	Company followers
New email sub-scribers	@ replies / mentions	Engaged users	+1 on content	Channel views	Shares
Comments	Direct messages	Page stories	Comments	Video views	Group members
Comment likes	Retweets	People talking about this	Mentions	Comments	Group discussions
Email to a friend	Brand-related hashtag mentions	Check-ins	Shares	Clicks on links shared	Clicks on links shared
Bookmark	Clicks on links shared	Clicks on links shared	Clicks on links shared	Site visits	Site visits
Shares to social networks	Site visits	Site visits	Site visits		
	Tweets favorited	Page and content likes			

Action/Conversion

The next stage in the new sales funnel is where most companies begin: action and conversion. This stage of the funnel is solely dedicated to qualified leads and those who go on to purchase your products or services. Regardless of which goal you select, if you do a good job of getting your brand in front of people and getting them to engage with you, sales will result. However, it is important to understand how lead generation in social media works and how it differs from other traditional advertising channels.

Social media leads are at a different stage in the buying cycle than people who have sought out your products or services with a search engine and clearly have a more immediate need. Social media leads tend to be earlier in the buying cycle, so they may take longer to convert. However, the benefit is that because you've engaged them, you are more likely to beat your competition to the prospect. If you do a good job of following up with appropriate content to push them through the sales cycle, and your product or service fills the need they have or solves their problem, they will be more likely to buy from you than from a competitor they haven't developed a relationship with. Your goal is to become the trusted vendor so that if all things are equal and your leads have a choice, they will select your company.

Two types of leads are generated through social media: leads who are ready to buy now, and those who have provided their contact information in exchange for a piece of high-value content you've made available. Those who have indicated they are interested in your products or services are called *hard leads* or *direct-response leads*. Those who have provided their contact information in exchange for non-product-related content are called *soft leads* or *indirect response leads*. If all goes well, both hard and soft leads will eventually purchase which is also measured. Chapter 5, "Social Media for Lead Generation," will go into a lot of detail about the social media lead, but for the purposes of this chapter, it is important to understand what metrics are used to measure this stage of the funnel. The table that follows provides the metrics that you can use to evaluate leads. Once you get to this stage in the funnel, the metrics are the same, but the response is evaluated independently for each social media channel.

	Blog	Twitter	Facebook	Google+	YouTube	LinkedIn
Soft leads						
Hard leads						
Customers						
Sales volume						
Revenue						

Customer Retention

The last stage of the sales funnel is customer retention. This is probably the most overlooked area of measurement for marketing channels. For some reason, once people get the customer, marketers tend to move on and forget to measure the customer's life cycle. Customer retention is a crucial piece in determining overall profitability of the customers you generate. Although a customer might interact with the social media channel during the sales process, it is important to understand that no customer is purely a social media customer. As with any marketing channel, social media is one piece of the puzzle. You can track customers who have interacted with the social channel throughout the customer life cycle to see whether there is a measurable difference in their activities. With all other things equal, it is reasonable to evaluate for trends based on the behavior of customers who interacted with the social media channel throughout their life cycle. Important considerations are how long social media customers stay customers, how much social media customers spend over time, how much it costs to serve social media customers, and how much new business is referred from social media customers.

Once prospects have become customers, you use different marketing activities to put them back into the top of the funnel, where they go through the buying stages to make their next purchase or add services. Although they go back into the funnel, they do tend to go through the stages much more quickly because there is already a familiarity with the brand and customer experience to draw on. If you kept them happy during their first experience, they are more likely to buy again.

You can make more money from existing customers in two core ways: encourage them to spend more at each transaction, or encourage them to purchase more frequently. Therefore, you perform two types of analysis for existing customers. You measure their repeat purchase activity, and you measure their effect on customer service resources. Because social media leads are generated online, with the right customer service strategies you can also encourage them to receive certain elements of customer service online, which can lower customer service costs. Similar to action and conversion, the metrics used to evaluate customer retention do not change with each channel; rather, you measure the performance of each channel to see whether one channel is performing better than another. For service providers, you look at the retention rate for customers or a measurement of how long they stay customers. This is especially important for companies that charge a monthly or annual fee. It is equally important for those who sell products to measure whether customers come back to purchase again. Chapter 8, "Measuring Strategies for Increasing Revenue from Existing Customers," goes into more detail about the metrics used to measure customer retention. The table that follows shows the core metrics for measuring customer retention for each of the social media networks used in the previous example.

	Blog	Twitter	Facebook	Google+	YouTube	LinkedIn
Retention rate						
Sales volume per customer						
Revenue per customer						
Customer service costs per customer						

The Path Through the Funnel

So, how does the funnel align with your actual activities in social media channels? Consider how someone might travel through the funnel:

Person A

1. Notices a retweet of a resource your company shared and took no action. (Exposure)

2. Sees a post Jason Falls wrote with a review of your products. (Influence)

3. Starts following your Twitter account and looks at some of your latest tweets. Sees a really great whitepaper, which he retweets to his audience. Goes to your website. (Engagement)

4. Fills out a form to download the whitepaper. (Action/Conversion, Soft Lead)

5. Sees that you have a webinar on Friday to explain your products. Decides to register. (Action/Conversion, Hard Lead)

6. Loves the webinar and what you have to offer. Decides to set up a meeting with the sales team. Fills out form on site to request times. (Action/Conversion, Hard Lead)

7. Has a meeting with your sales representative and decides the company need your product. Makes a purchase. (Action/Conversion Hard Lead)

8. Loves your product. Follows your social channels to keep up-to-date with the company. Sees a tweet for a free trial of an add-on product he's been considering. Clicks on the link and goes to your site. (Engagement)

9. Fills out the form for the free trial. (Action/Conversion, Hard Lead)

10. Loves the add-on and adds it to his account. (Action/Conversion, Hard Lead)

In this example, you see that Person A went through all the stages of the funnel. After he made the purchase, he became an active prospect for an add-on product and went through the last three stages again during the purchase. It is important to recognize that people can come into the funnel at any stage. They can also fall out of the funnel at any stage. The funnel displays an ongoing relationship with prospects as well as with customers. After the initial purchase is made, the relationship doesn't end. Further, it is possible to skip stages in the funnel. The funnel isn't gated so that people can't move ahead without getting through the last stage. Rather, the funnel represents "potential" areas where prospects and customers might engage in a measureable way. As you measure the funnel, you will be able to identify where you are losing people and where you are doing well. This will be covered in depth in Chapter 5.

Whichever goal you selected in Chapter 1, "Aligning Social Media Strategies to Business Goals," the funnel still applies. The five categories align with the three goals, but their purpose is a little different. If your goal is customer retention and you do your job well, you will notice that more sales result from existing customers. This means that you are effectively placing people back into the top of the funnel, even if they follow a different path than a prospective customer would take. Have you set yourself up to measure it?

Social Media Is the Assist

You'll also notice that in the previous example, all the interaction happened on the social media channel. A lot of people will tell you that social media is the end-all, be-all channel. They will tell you that your company will no longer be relevant if you don't dump your marketing budget into social media right now. Social media is one communication channel of many that can be just as important to your business as public relations, advertising, email marketing, direct mail. To best understand where social media fits into the overall marketing picture, think about the actual path your prospects and customers will take. Is it realistic to assume that if a prospect interacts with the social media team, no other marketing channel will be used to communicate with him? Absolutely not. What is more likely is that you will have interactions in the social media channel and several others. Should you keep those who interact with the social media team from going into campaigns in other channels? Heck, no. Why would you want to be responsible for creating an entirely new end-to-end communication channel? That is a lot of unnecessary work. A more likely interaction path is the one that follows.

Person B

1. Notices a retweet with a resource your company shared and takes no action. (Exposure)

2. Sees a post Jason Falls wrote with a review of your products. (Influence)

3. Starts following your Twitter account and looks at some of your latest tweets. Sees a really great whitepaper, which she retweets to her audience. Goes to your website. (Engagement)

4. Fills out a form to download the whitepaper. (Action/Conversion, Soft Lead)

5. Receives several emails from the company sharing additional content. Sees another piece of content that is interesting and looks at it. (Action/Conversion, Soft Lead)

6. Receives an email with a downloadable guide for selecting the best product to serve her needs. Downloads the guide. (Action/Conversion, Hard Lead)

7. Receives a phone call from the sales team asking if she'd like to see a demonstration of your product. Sets up a meeting. (Action/Conversion, Hard Lead)

8. Sees the demo of your product. Decides she likes it but isn't ready to buy yet. (Action/Conversion, Hard Lead)

9. Receives several emails with special offers for the product. When ready to buy, clicks on the latest offer she received. (Action/Conversion, Hard Lead)

10. Receives emails about how to use your product. Clicks through some of the resources. (Engagement)

11. Continues to follow your social channels to keep up to date with the company. Sees a tweet for a free trial of an add-on product she's been considering. Clicks on the link and goes to your site. (Engagement)

12. Fills out the form for the free trial. (Action/Conversion, Hard Lead)

13. Loves the add-on and adds it to her account. (Action/Conversion, Hard Lead)

One of your primary goals for social media should be to put as many people into your existing marketing communications channels as possible. You might need to reframe your point of reference for where social media adds the most value. Social media is one method of communication. It can be really great at bringing opportunities to the table, but existing marketing programs for handling leads are where the customer is most likely converted. Social media is effective at raising awareness of the brand, bringing leads to the table, and interacting with customers, but it is not an end-to-end communications vehicle. For example, if you have an ongoing webinar series, you want to get social media followers to register for the webinars and then be part of the email campaigns that work to convert webinar attendees into customers. Social media is effective at bringing more opportunities to the table, but it can also be effective at taking existing opportunities to the next stage. A solid social media strategy will recognize where social media creates opportunities, where it adds value to existing opportunities, and, most importantly, where it doesn't fit.

Think of your marketing channels as if they were a basketball team. You have a point guard responsible for calling the plays and leading the team. You have a shooting guard focused on getting the ball to the basket, either himself or by passing to other players. Then you have the center, power forward, and small forward responsible for shooting and getting rebounds from missed shots. Social media can be any of these positions, but the position it plays least often is the point guard. Rather, social media falls into the shooting guard position most often. Sometimes it receives a pass from another channel and drives it to the basket, sometimes it powers the ball down the court on its own and hits a nice three-pointer, and many times it delivers a great pass to the center for a crowd-pleasing slam dunk.

More often than not, social media is the almighty assist. It provides a fantastic pass to another marketing channel, or it takes a pass and drives it to the basket. Sure, social media can also take the ball down the court and score on its own occasionally. But the difference between this analogy and real social media is that the ball in social media is a person with free will. As a social media professional, you have to respond to the needs of the audience and present as many opportunities for them to convert through other channels as possible. This requires that you review the communications your company uses at every stage of the funnel to see whether they work with social media contacts. In lead generation, for example, many times a company has great email campaigns built for someone who is ready to buy, but it doesn't have anything built for those who aren't quite there yet. Finding these weaknesses early is important to the overall success of your program.

Measuring Through the Funnel

How do you know where people are in the sales funnel? How do you know if you are having an impact? To effectively measure where people are, you need to put some tracking mechanisms in place. You'll see exactly how to do that later. However, there are a few caveats to measuring through the funnel that are important to understand.

Measuring Multiple Touches

Social media leads are going to touch multiple marketing channels. This might affect your ability to show where social media had an "assist." Many existing tracking systems measure the last touch as the campaign that drove the sale but neglect to recognize all the channels that contributed to the sale. Google Analytics recognized this and has attempted to help solve this problem with their new social reports dashboard, which shows both the social media assist and the social media conversion. You need to understand how your systems attribute credit so that you can effectively measure social media's touches. Many times, this means you have to make some concessions for things that you can't measure today. But the one big thing you need to be able to tell is whether someone touched the social media channel.

Measuring a Control Group

The best way to show where social media is contributing is to have a way to isolate all the customers in your customer relationship management (CRM) system who have touched the social media channel. This creates a control group that you can use to compare the results from social media to the general population. This adds another layer of credibility to your data because you can demonstrate the differences from those who came through the social media channel from those who came through other marketing channels. Initially, the social media channel may not have numbers that excite the management team. It takes time to build a social media following that is engaged enough to deliver the type of volume that has taken years to build on other marketing channels. If you don't measure a control group, the management team may brush off social media as an underperforming channel. However, when you measure a control group, you can show where social media is outperforming other channels, where it is helping other marketing channels perform more efficiently, and where it is filling the gaps where other channels can't effectively demonstrate value.

This isn't about showing that social media is better than other marketing channels or that social media is a silver bullet that solves all marketing problems. Rather, it is having the data you need to demonstrate how social media complements and integrates into other marketing channels. You'll see how this comes into play when later chapters examine in-depth case studies. But for now, you need to be able to source new and returning interest back to the marketing channel that originated, nurtured, and converted the interest.

Hands-On Exercise: Aligning the Funnel with Communications

The communication that prospects and customers receive through the funnel is important. If the communications you are using today will not facilitate a deeper relationship with social media contacts, adjust them so they don't kill the relationship. This exercise evaluates your communications campaigns at each stage of the funnel (see Figure 2.2).

Figure 2.2 *Sales funnel communications worksheet*

Activity 1: Chart Existing Communications

Next to each stage in the funnel, write the existing communications that a social media contact could receive. This should include any form of communication that goes directly to the social media contact, including emails, phone calls, direct mail, and any other product your team uses. You want to understand every potential touch to see whether it is relationship-building or relationship-killing for those who came through social media.

Activity 2: Identify Communications Pieces That Don't Work With Contacts Who Touched the Social Media Channel

Do any communications make you cringe when you think about a social media contact receiving it? Are any communications designed for people who might not be interested in your products or service yet? Are some communications designed to keep your company top of mind without being overly pushy toward a sale? If there is anything you see on this list that makes you uncomfortable, think about how it could be adjusted to solve the problem. You might need to create new communications pieces, or you might need to apply a few simple tweaks to make something more appropriate.

Problem Communication Piece	Ideas to Adjust

Activity 3: Determine Metrics to Evaluate Where People Fall Out of the Funnel

Now that you have an idea of how existing communication channels align with social media, you need to understand how to evaluate whether the existing communications are helping or hurting the relationship. Use the following table to think about the metrics you could monitor to determine where people are falling out of the funnel. Here are some ideas to help get you started.

Email Campaigns: # of Unsubscribes, # of Opens, # of Clicks

If you notice that social media contacts are unsubscribing at a higher rate, stop opening the emails at a certain point, or even stop clicking on links, it is a good sign that they are falling out of the funnel. Communication needs to be adjusted.

Sales Phone Calls: # of Follow-Ups Created, # of Sales

If calls from the sales team aren't resulting in follow-up opportunities or generating sales, it is likely that these calls are not helping to deepen the relationship. These calls might be happening too early in the buying process for the social media lead.

Communication	Metrics to Measure Fall-Off	Notes

Do you have a mechanism to collect these metrics easily? Can you isolate the social media group from the rest of the population? If not, it's okay. This book reviews how to overcome the barriers later, but it's important to recognize early the areas where the gaps exist.

3

Social Media for Brand Awareness

Arguably, brand awareness has the longest history in marketing teams. It may even be the primary reason marketing teams were created—awareness was the one thing that salespeople couldn't produce. In the hit TV show Mad Men, which focuses on an early advertising agency, brand awareness campaigns abound. Traditionally, they focus on catchy TV ads, radio spots, public relations outreach, print advertising, and direct mail. Big brands spend billions of dollars just for the possibility that you might remember their name. Because social media costs are pennies on the dollar compared to traditional media, it isn't surprising to see companies working to leverage social media to boost brand awareness.

Reality Check No. 1: No One Cares About Your Brand

You have fallen in love with your brand, and you assume that the world has, too. In reality, your audience probably doesn't wake up and think, "I can't wait to see what (your name here) is going to post on Facebook today!" Companies have tried to use social media networks in the same way they use other marketing channels: to control and push their messages out to the world. But if you build a social media strategy around talking about your brand, it's more likely to fail. Why? Because people don't really care about your brand and don't want to engage with it. People care about people; that's who they want to engage with. If you want to grow a loyal social media audience, you have to match the marketing medium with the purpose. Social media is about connecting with people; so do a better job of putting people in front of the brand. Accept that people don't care about your brand unless you give them a compelling reason to care.

Digital strategist Mike Arauz had visionary insight in March 2009 when he said, "If I tell my Facebook friends about your brand, it's not because I like your brand, but rather because I like my friends."

This isn't to say that a company's brand isn't important. Branding is incredibly important for both B2B and B2C companies. The difference is how important you think your brand is versus how important your brand is to your audience. If you think you can set up a Facebook page and your audience is going to flock to become a fan of your brand, because after all, your brand is so cool, you may be extremely disappointed with the results. In social media, traditional brand messaging doesn't translate with the type of relationships that audiences want with social brands. There is a big difference to what is important to how a consumer brand is represented in 7-11 and how the same brand is represented in social media. In social media, it is important to humanize the brand and show brand personality because individuals use social networks to build and deepen relationships. Ultimately, the reality is that in social media no one cares about the brand; rather, your audience cares about the relationship with the brand. The value proposition is different—you need to focus on what value they will receive by taking the opportunity to deepen their relationship with the team behind the brand and therefore the brand itself.

Reality Check No. 2: You Have Lost Control of Your Brand

Many marketers will try to develop a brand awareness strategy so they can "control the message." You are going to have to accept, however, that you have officially lost control of your brand. Your prospects and customers have it now. They tell people what they think you do and whether you do it well; and those people listen. Social media has given them the platform to spread their word quickly, and with tremendous reach.

When your audience loves you social media reach can be a game changer even for small companies. Dollar Shave Club used a funny video with a nice taste of edge to spread the word about its subscription razor company that resulted in 600,000 views in 2 days and more than 5,000 orders. If you haven't seen the video, seriously, stop and do a search. Dollar Shave Club is a great example of how brand messaging can translate into social media. It didn't focus on boring positioning such as, "we give you the best value in disposable razors." Rather, they said exactly what was on their minds: "Our razors are F***ing Great!" When you visit their site you see there was a clear and cohesive brand message strategy that flows through everything they do. It is compelling and site visitors share it with their friends, a lot.

This is a tough pill to swallow, especially at the chief marketing officer level. Marketers have built their careers around the notion that their job is to control the message. They have frightened CEOs with the dangers of letting "others" decide how to communicate the company message. When that is stripped away, they fear that they have no purpose—that their jobs are being stolen by a thief in the night. Their greatest fear—losing control of the message—has become a reality, and they have no idea how to explain it to their CEOs (whom they have convinced that this loss of control signifies Armageddon). Fortunately, it isn't quite as bad as all that. Although your audience may now have a readily available platform to say what they think about your company, it hasn't rendered you helpless. Your job in brand control has simply evolved. You can spend less time being brand police and more time working to influence brand perceptions, to gently correct misperceptions, and to fiercely fix your mistakes with customers who have negative experiences. While you may have lost brand control, you now have an even greater opportunity to use your talents in brand influence.

Where Brand Awareness Fits into the Funnel

Brand awareness is represented in the first three stages of the new sales funnel. You could consider it the beginning of the lead generation process. Whether you're deploying brand awareness campaigns or not, the reality is that brand awareness is the first stage of every purchase. Buyers must first discover that your company exists. Then they can consider whether your product or service is a good fit for their needs. By devising a strategic approach to brand awareness, you're extending the sales funnel and providing more sales opportunities for your company. Even though brand awareness campaigns may not be specifically designed to generate sales, the net effect is that they will create opportunities that will contribute to sales through the pipeline.

Types of Brand Awareness

Two types of brand awareness relate to social media: brand awareness campaigns and reputation management. Brand awareness campaigns are about helping your brand become "memorable" to your target audience. They're focused on making it easier for customers to remember the name of your brand and where they've seen it. This isn't easy. How many times have you watched a commercial, thought it was hilarious, and then couldn't remember the brand behind it? Even a catchy ad can fall flat when it comes to brand recall. So marketers try different types of campaigns: those that inspire emotion, those that make people laugh, and even those with annoying jingles that you can't get out of your head.

The other brand awareness focus is reputation management. Reputation management works to ensure that your brand has a positive reputation in the marketplace and that negative publicity is minimized. It's a lot like a marriage: brand managers have to be up for managing good media coverage and, sometimes more importantly, for managing the bad. This can be tough because negative publicity is usually unexpected, and many teams are unprepared to respond. The best teams have detailed crisis management plans detailing exactly how their organizations will respond to negative media coverage, including boilerplate language that can be customized to an event and designating who is responsible for which tasks. They may even run practice drills to ensure that they're ready to handle an emergency. If you haven't practiced managing a publicity crisis, you'll be unprepared to handle one elegantly.

Where Social Media Fits into Brand Awareness Campaigns

Social media has provided a cost-effective way for companies of all sizes to generate brand awareness. It allows smaller companies to build brand loyalty at a fraction of

> *A CEO is ultimately responsible for the growth of a company as evidenced by its financial performance, its capacity for self-renewal, and its character. The only way you can measure character is by reputation.*
>
> —Former Coca-Cola CEO Roberto Goizueta

the budget that big brands spend on advertising campaigns. Earlier, you saw the example of King Arthur Flour, which has developed a loyal following by providing value to its audience with social media. King Arthur isn't your traditional advertiser that spends millions on TV ads in hopes that you will remember its flour at the grocery store. But with social media, King Arthur has captured its audience's attention with a budget it can afford.

The Original Wine of the Month Club is another good example of how to use social media to develop brand awareness. It leverages social media to have conversations with fans; it makes the act of enjoying wine something anyone can do, not something restricted to pretentious wine connoisseurs.

On the Original Wine of the Month Club's pages, you will see everything from funny anecdotes about wine to tips on how to develop your tasting preferences (see Figure 3.1).

Figure 3.1   *Wine of the Month Club uses humor, educational information, and promotions to increase brand awareness.*

Even big companies are finding social media an effective outlet to augment their traditional brand awareness campaigns. Many of these companies use social media to support their TV and radio campaigns by extending existing promotions to the digital channel. A fantastic example of an integrated campaign was Old Spice's Isaiah Mustafa campaign, which extended the company's TV commercials by creating funny YouTube videos of Mustafa talking to other famous people and responding to Twitter comments (see Figure 3.2). These videos went viral and have accumulated millions of views since the campaign launched. That exposure helped reposition Old Spice and changed the way consumers perceived its products. Old Spice once was considered a brand for older gentlemen, but this campaign helped refresh the company's image and attract a younger demographic to its products. And it worked. Adweek's Eleftheria Parpis reported in July 2010 shortly after the campaign launch: "According to Nielsen data provided by Old Spice, overall sales for Old Spice body-wash products are up 11% in the last 12 months; up 27% in the last six months; up 55% in the last three months; and in the last month, with two new TV spots and the online response videos, up a whopping 107%."[1]

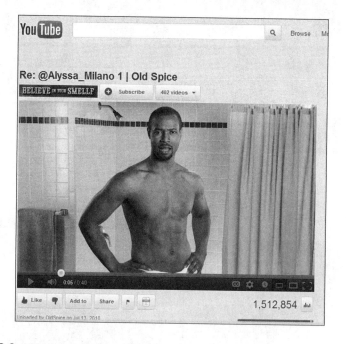

Figure 3.2 *Old Spice repositioned its brand with the Mustafa social media campaign.*

1. http://www.adweek.com/adfreak/hey-old-spice-haters-sales-are-107-12422

As in traditional advertising, creating an intentionally "viral" campaign is extremely difficult, if not impossible. It's tough to predict what will catch on and how audiences will respond—simply making a funny video doesn't guarantee success. Brands that are focused on providing consistent value and developing trust rather than fleeting top-of-mind interest are finding that they can readily predict the success of their content based upon its value to the audience.

Matt Grant, managing editor for MarketingProfs, is using an interesting philosophy for how the company evaluates its content. He said, "When we create content we ask ourselves, 'Is this content good enough to sell?' Even if we plan on giving away the content for free, we've decided that if the audience wouldn't actually pay for our marketing content, then it isn't good enough." That's a whole new spin on content creation in the social channel. Suddenly, "getting your message out" becomes "put out a tremendous amount of value," and your message becomes secondary.

Where does social media fit into brand awareness campaigns? It provides a level playing field for businesses of all sizes; it creates a tremendous opportunity for cross-channel campaigns, and it forces brands to be strategic about their content for the social channel.

Where Social Media Fits into Reputation Management

Social media has made reputation management more difficult for marketing teams because in the past five years it has dramatically increased the number of people who can, in an instant, publish positive and negative stories about your company. Media coverage is no longer limited to traditional news outlets. Today, it's necessary to monitor blogs, Twitter updates, Facebook pages, YouTube channels, Google+ updates, forums, and online communities that are a playground of positive and negative mentions for brands. Further, the ability for a story to go "viral"—with or without traditional media coverage—has risen dramatically. More than ever, consumers have the power to share news that is important to them. If they're saying nice things about your brand, great! But if they're saying negative things about you, it can be extremely detrimental.

Social media has been credited for breaking news stories, launching music stars, and even fueling a revolution. If it has that kind of power, it can certainly energize an awesome brand that uses it well—and destroy a brand that mishandles negativity. Netflix made this mistake (see Figure 3.3). On July 12, 2011, it announced on its blog and in an email to customers that it was increasing its subscription rates by more than 60%. This was veiled in a message stating they were separating their DVD and streaming services. Customers who had the $9.99 bundle that included both would have to pay separately at a cost of $16. Immediately, customers complained furiously on Netflix's blog and Facebook page. The company didn't respond to a single comment—which infuriated its customers even more. Two months later (two months!), Netflix posted an apology video that was met with more than 5,000 dislikes and fewer than 800 likes. Viewers posted over and over that they didn't feel the apology was genuine and that the CEO appeared smug. In the video, Netflix CEO Reed Hastings made a common mistake: He described how the price increase would benefit Netflix; he didn't explain how the separation of its DVD service would benefit customers. He said that with a separate brand, the company could have a separate website and a separate fulfillment service and advertise separately. Although this may have made operations easier for the company, for the customer it meant going to two websites and paying two fees. This misalignment cost Netflix. During the quarter when the company made the announcement, it lost 800,000 subscribers. Netflix is still working to regain ground.[2]

Figure 3.3   *Netflix apologizes, kind of.*

Something else that has changed the approach to reputation management is that the online conversation happens and spreads in real time. This probably is why so many Netflix customers were angered that it took two months for Netflix to

2. http://www.bloomberg.com/news/2011-10-24/netflix-3q-subscriber-losses-worse-than-forecast.html

respond to its concerns. When a story takes off, it can require an all-hands-on-deck approach to sort through the conversations and create an appropriate and timely response.

The old days of lying low, staying quiet, and waiting for a crisis to die down have disappeared. Now the best response is proactive and transparent. Southwest has done a good job of mitigating negative press, with its responses to the "too pretty to fly" and "too fat to fly" controversies that have cropped up. The company was transparent, apologetic, and human in its responses.

Kevin Smith tweeted, "Dear @SouthwestAir - I know I'm fat, but was Captain Leysath really justified in throwing me off a flight for which I was already seated?"

Southwest responded, "I've read the tweets all night from @thatkevinsmith - He'll be getting a call at home from our Customer Relations VP tonight," it tweeted. "Again, I'm very sorry for the experience you had tonight. Please let me know if there is anything else I can do."

Tone is extremely important in social media, and scripted talking heads won't help a brand regain its footing.

Where does social media fit into reputation management? It flips traditional reputation management on its head and requires teams to mobilize quickly, respond honestly, and lose the spin. Spin won't fly on social channels. Consumers have developed extremely sensitive bull detectors.

Developing a Measureable Strategy for a Brand Awareness Campaign

If your primary goal for social media is brand awareness, you need to find a way to capture the interest of your target market. The best way to do that is to understand what they care about, why they use social media, and how you can create a compelling conversation. To do this, you'll need to spend some time understanding your audience. Too many companies start their social media strategies by randomly opening a Facebook or Twitter account, without taking the time to truly understand their audience.

Create a Listening Station

If you've read other social media books, you've probably heard this preached at you 100 different ways, but it's a crucial element to developing any social media strategy—you can't do your job effectively if you don't know what's being said about you. Your first step is to create a list of keywords that identify relevant conversations about your brand, your competition, and your industry. The second is to deploy one or more tools to collect that data for you. Several tools in the market can make listening easier: Radian6, Sysomos, HootSuite, Spiral16, and Google Alerts are a few. Each of these tools has varying capabilities to monitor conversations related to the list of keywords you've selected. For small budgets, Google Alerts can be a great start to understanding how your brand is mentioned online, but it tends to miss mentions on social channels like Twitter and Facebook. Overall, listening to these conversations requires an assortment of tools to make sure you're hearing everything. Your budget will be a big factor in the sophistication and effectiveness of your listening station. The difference in capabilities from one tool to the next reflects in their price differences.

Interpret the Conversation

After you've been listening for a few weeks, look at the conversations you've found. What are people saying about your brand? What are they saying about your competition? What are they saying about the industry? There are a few things you want to look for while evaluating these conversations.

Brand Sentiment

The first thing you want to understand is how people feel about your brand. Are people saying good things? Are they saying negative things? Or are they saying nothing at all? If people are saying good things, your role is to find a way to broaden the reach of those messages. If people are saying negative things, your job is to help turn complaints into raves. If people are saying nothing, your job is to give them a reason to talk about you.

Competitor Sentiment

Next, you want to understand what the audience is saying about your competition. Ask yourself the same questions as in the previous section: are the comments negative, positive, or nonexistent? It's common to realize that one of your competitors is dominating online conversations. You'll want to understand where you stack up to the competition, good or bad. Another great thing to evaluate during this stage is what your competitors are doing well in social channels and where they're falling flat. If they've beaten you to the social media channel, at least you can learn from what they've already tried.

Industry Conversation Analysis

Although conversations about your brand and your competition can be extremely enlightening, you may find the real gems in conversations about your industry.

These are conversations that mention key industry term words but do not contain your brand or your competitor's brand names. These conversations will provide a sampling of the types of questions your audience has, insight into how they make purchasing decisions, and their general sentiment toward the industry.

Why Listening Matters

Listening gives you the knowledge to create the right type of content at the right time, and it empowers you to distribute it to the right places. By understanding existing conversations, you can create a database of questions that have been asked, you can understand how your audience makes a decision to purchase your product, and you can understand how they feel about your industry. This can fuel an extremely powerful content calendar that answers the most important questions your audience has. Marketers often make the mistake of thinking they understand their audience. A listening audit is a crucial step toward making sure you know as much as you think you do.

Refine Your Brand Awareness Goal

Generating brand awareness likely is too big a task to accomplish with a singular strategy. Start instead by breaking brand awareness into subgoals that define exactly what you hope to achieve with your brand awareness strategies. For example, if you're hoping to drive website traffic, it's important that your strategy includes a clear call to action to go to the website. However, if one of your goals is to create a Facebook community that helps each other and shares ideas, you'll want to make sure your strategy includes tactics that inspire more user-generated content on the page. Think about what a successful brand awareness strategy would look like, and ask yourself what actions your audience would have to take for it to be deemed a success. The goal is to come away from this exercise with three or four subgoals to drive strategy creation.

Define Niches Within Your Target Market

Most companies feel that they have their target market figured out. For example, most consumer demographic targeting includes the gender, age, and income level of the audience, such as: "We're targeting female consumers between the ages of 18 and 35 who earn between $45k and $80k per year." This is actually a common target demographic that companies use to create marketing strategies. In social media, however, that's a wide audience with myriad needs, interests, and values. Although you can try to be everything to everyone, it's wise to focus initially on a smaller target market. More narrowly defined target audiences are critical for social media because it is important to break out of the clutter. One simple way to stand out is to ensure you can effectively speak directly to an audience's needs. Loosely defined target audiences are too diverse to be able to communicate directly to their needs. But when you narrow your focus you can personalize your content directly to the needs of the audience. You can also have several niche targets and create content specifically for each one. Just make sure that you align the niches with the best potential for downstream revenue and that you don't bite off more than you can chew by picking too many. You can consider several areas for using niche targeting within your social media strategy.

Examples of Consumer Niches

- Marital status
- Parent/Nonparent
- Specific interests
- Life stage

The life stage of the audience can be interesting for developing a targeted strategy. Think about the varying needs of a young adult going into his first job versus the needs of a mother whose children are in high school. These life stages have different challenges that merit completely different sets of content in the social media channel. If you can home in on a couple of niches that align well with when your product or service would be useful to them, you can create hyper-targeted content that is extremely relevant to the audience. You also can create a list of social media influencers who already have the attention of those audiences and work to build relationships with them to distribute content they will find useful.

Examples of B2B Niches

In the business-to-business (B2B) world, audiences are commonly defined by the size of the business—in revenue or the number of employees. "We are targeting businesses that have less than $5 million in revenue with fewer than 10 employees," for example. However, this is a wide audience that has several differentiators. If you look at the companies that would fit in that demographic, you could find a B2B software company, a government contracting firm, and a small boutique retailer. Their needs and what they care about are drastically different. Consider refining your target to include high-value industries where your products are useful. For example, you could create a strategy around B2B software companies that includes information on the challenges of getting new users and keeping existing users happy while growing revenue—that would be hyper-relevant to the audience. There are influencers in the B2B software space that have earned high levels of trust among other B2B software companies and commonly produce content for the industry. The important distinction from the consumer area here is that an influencer in B2B software is someone who influences other software companies in the industry. This may be drastically different from the B2B software CEO who has a strong following of users of the company's own product.

When you've defined a couple of high-value niche audiences, start building successful strategies. It's important to align strategies with how you will measure them early because that's the difference between a measureable and a nonmeasureable strategy.

Define Social Media Channels

Through your listening strategy, you should have seen which social networks your customers frequent. Now it's important to refine your searches to include the niche audience(s) you've decided to target. Are they all over Twitter, or do they spend their time in community forums? Either way, make a list of the social networks you see your audience participating in and rank them based on the level of activity. Then pick one channel. (You will be tempted to try a cross-channel campaign right out of the gate, but remember it is important to test first.) Test in one channel and see if you get any traction. If you do, you can expand into other channels.

Social media relies on content to be successful, so for your campaign to work, you need to produce awesome content. This requires some kind of a blog or web pages within your content management system that you can easily and quickly post content on. You want to drive people to your blog, but you should participate in another network to start the relationship. If people were already looking for you, they would've already found your blog. Your campaign will seek to get the attention of people who didn't know you exist.

Define Success Metrics

Before your head starts swimming with ideas, think about what success looks like. What metrics will you measure? What metrics matter? How will you show an impact on the bottom line?

Let's review the brand awareness metrics from Chapter 2, "Aligning Social Media to the Sales Funnel."

Exposure Metrics			
Twitter	Facebook	YouTube	LinkedIn
Impressions from content	Total reach	Channel views	Displayed in search results

Influence Metrics					
Calculated from the Reach of Influencers Who Mention the Brand Only on the Networks On Which the Brand Was Mentioned					
Blog	**Twitter**	**Facebook**	**Google+**	**YouTube**	**LinkedIn**
RSS subscribers	Followers	Fans	Followers	Channel subscribers	Connections
Average monthly site traffic	Followers of those who retweet post	Friends of those who engage	Followers of those who +1		

Engagement Metrics					
Blog	**Twitter**	**Facebook**	**Google+**	**YouTube**	**LinkedIn**
RSS subscribers	Followers	Fans	Followers	Subscribers	Company followers
New email subscribers	@ replies mentions	Engaged users	+1 on content	Channel views	Shares
Comments	Direct messages	Page stories	Comments	Video views	Group members
Comment likes	Retweets	People talking about this	Mentions	Comments	Group discussions
Email to a friend	Brand-related hashtag mentions	Check-ins	Shares	Clicks on links shared	Clicks on links shared
Bookmark	Clicks on links shared	Clicks on links shared	Clicks on links shared	Site visits	Site visits
	Site visits	Site visits	Site visits		

Clearly, that's a lot of metrics. The big question is this: What do you want your strategy to accomplish? Gathering a bunch of fans who don't engage or convert into anything is unlikely to impress your management team. Think instead about how a brand awareness campaign could "convert." Is there a type of conversion the company feels is most valuable? What about email subscribers? If you convert fans and followers into email subscribers, you obtain contact information that you can use for follow-up campaigns. Whatever type of metric it is, make sure it is tangible and your management team understands it. Find three or four for these metrics you can hold up as defining success for a campaign. Hint: Impressions aren't one. Most likely, success will revolve around site visits and email subscribers because these show a transition from the social channel into direct engagement with the company.

Define Your Strategy

Now that you know who you want to target, where you want to target them, and how you will measure success, define your strategy. A lot of marketers will jump into tactics at this stage. That is not a strategy, and it can be a recipe for a lackluster performance. A strategy is who you are targeting and what you want to accomplish. It doesn't say how, and it doesn't say that you are using social media to do it. That's a big differentiator. As times and needs change in business, many times the strategy doesn't change, but the tactics used to achieve it do. This book happens to be evaluating social media, but your strategy could combine traditional media, PR, direct mail, and social media. In fact, the best and most successful strategies will use an integrated approach.

Example Strategy A:

Generate product awareness with new mothers

Example Strategy B:

Generate product awareness with B2B software companies that earn less than $5 million in revenue and have fewer than 10 employees

Does that look a little generic to you? It should. A strategy defines what you're trying to accomplish and is a guide for ensuring that your campaign is working to achieve it. Once you're brainstorming campaign ideas, you can check it against your strategy to make sure they're on target with what you're trying to accomplish. These strategies may be tweaked over the years—you may decide to do something beyond increasing email subscribers—but the core piece of the strategy "Generate product awareness with new mothers" and "Generate product awareness with B2B software companies" is less likely to change drastically unless you find that the strategies aren't designed for a viable audience for your product or service.

Define How You Will Do It

Now it's time for the fun part—running rampant with ideas. Everyone loves this part, and it's often the starting point. But by going through the process first, you've gained guard rails to work within that will ultimately help your ideas be more successful. Brainstorm about how you can attract your audience, what type of content they care about, where you should share this content, and how you can develop relationships and partnerships with influencers.

Write down your ideas; there are no wrong answers at this stage. When you've exhausted your creativity, look at those ideas and immediately strike any that don't align with your strategy. They may be good for another day, but they aren't good for this. From what you have left, do any of the ideas rise to the top? Use the following criteria to organize and prioritize your ideas.

1. Does the idea deliver on the strategy?

2. How likely is the audience to respond to this idea compared to the others?

3. Do we have the resources to implement this idea, either ourselves or with a contractor?

4. Are there any roadblocks to this idea?

What bubbled to the top? Many times some of the ideas that are cool and sexy at the beginning don't fit the bill after this test.

Flesh It Out

Flesh out the top two or three ideas and see where you land. Although you may only roll with one or two to start with, sometimes as you lay out your execution plan you find that one of the ideas becomes implausible. So it's best to work on two or three. If your first idea works well, you can justify implementing the other two. If you have the resources to test three or four ideas at a time, awesome. You'll likely find the successful campaign earlier.

Developing a Measureable Strategy for Reputation Management

A strategy for reputation management is drastically different from a brand awareness campaign. With a brand awareness campaign you can be proactive, but reputation management has both proactive and reactive components. Luckily, the steps to build your strategy are similar.

Develop a Listening Station

Listening plays an even more important role in reputation management. It's the central point where you receive information about what's being said about your brand, industry, and competitors. The first step is to gain understanding of what already has been said. Follow the steps for developing a listening station that were reviewed with the brand awareness campaigns. For reputation management, it's even more important to monitor for sentiment: How do consumers feel about your brand, your products or services, your industry, and your competition? Are there any obvious potential stressors for the audience? Is there praise you can highlight and publicize? How do consumers feel about your competitors? Do they love or hate them more than they do you? Do they feel their products or services are better? Understanding how the audience views your brand and your competitors' brands is important for developing a campaign to either correct misperceptions or highlight your positive image. Sentiment analysis is difficult to automate, and while many social media monitoring tools claim they do it the best, it is worth running a test in their tool and manually reviewing the results. Radian6 and Sysomos have two of the most accurate sentiment engines, but a manual check will always be required for any tool.

Outline the Types of Reputation Management You Will Focus On

Because reputation management is proactive and reactive, it's important to outline the types of reputation management. This outline will help you determine what type of training, policies, and content you'll need.

Some of the types of reputation management you might want to be prepared for are discussed next.

Negative Press Coverage

Every company should have a plan for handling a media attack on its brand. The plan should include how to respond, who will respond, and what the process is to get the approval to respond. Once those are decided, run several mock exercises in which you actually use the plan. David B. Thomas, Director of Community and Social Strategy for Salesforce Radian6, recommends that you not only do "fire drills" as he calls them, but that you do them in the evenings or on weekends when people aren't in the office. This will help your team identify gaps in the process.

Customer Complaint

You'll also want to prepare for handling a customer complaint on a social network. Managing complaints online is an art form. It requires that someone respond who really understands not only customer service, but the importance of tone when online. Write a document detailing the expectations for the employee who is responding online and sample responses that can be used as a framework for content and tone. What is the company's stance on responding? What if the customer continues to respond? When do you respond, and when do you ignore a complaint? What guidelines should be followed when responding?

Positive Mention by Media or Customer

It's equally important to have a plan for handling positive mentions. Some brands simply can't respond to every positive mention of their brand, whereas other companies make it a top priority to respond to every mention. How will your company handle positive mentions? Do you respond with, "Thank you for the kind words," or do you craft individual responses?

Conversations That Are Relevant to Your Audience

Reputation management is more than watching to see if someone talks about your brand. You also have to monitor conversations that are relevant to your industry, your products or services, and your target customers. You can add value to these conversations and engage an audience that otherwise might not know about your company.

Create Social Media Accounts Before You Need Them

In a reputation management strategy, the existing conversation about your brand will largely dictate which networks you participate in. Another great tip from David B. Thomas is to create your social media accounts before you need them. Set up accounts on the networks where you see activity around your industry or brand. Be sure to monitor this chatter, and if you see a relevant conversation on a new network, set up a presence. There are two things to consider in this section. First, what type of presence will you have, and will you publish brand-building content through those channels? If you participate in these channels, you have the opportunity to build a loyal following that can help combat negative coverage by coming to your defense. Second, what policy will you have about setting up a new social network? Having corporate identities in the social world can proliferate out of control quickly, so write a policy that shows what needs to happen before you start a new account.

Define Success Metrics

How will you evaluate whether the effort you're putting into reputation management is worth it? What metrics will you present to your management team to show that this is important for the company? There are some metrics that can come into play with reputation management that aren't specific to certain networks.

Reputation Management Metrics	
Save Rate	What's your success rate for saving clients who could have left?
Response Rate	How long does it take your team to respond?
Share of Voice	What percentage of the conversations are about your brand, your competitors' brands, and about the industry?
Sentiment	Of all the conversations, what percent is positive or neutral, and what percent is negative?
Complaint Rate	In a crisis, you can measure how many of your customers complain compared to how many were affected by the issue.

Define Your Strategy

Next, define your strategy. Just because reputation management can be reactive doesn't mean you don't have goals and a clear strategy to reach them. Think about your strategy for being reactive and what you can do to be proactive to create a positive image for the brand.

Example Strategy A:

Protect the company's reputation by monitoring and responding to positive and negative mentions of the brand in social media channels.

Example Strategy B:

Proactively generate positive sentiment for the brand by sharing relevant content that the audience will respond to.

Your strategy should focus on what you want to accomplish with reputation management. Consider what approach you will use when a reactive response is required. Consider what approach you would take to proactively generate positive sentiment around your brand. In addition to addressing your primary goal, all strategies should include a component dedicated to how you would manage a communications crisis.

Define How You Will Do It

Now you can brainstorm how you will manage the company's reputation. Consider types of campaigns that could increase the positive perception of the brand. Consider which resources you need to monitor the results and which policies you need to create. Put together a list of ideas for how you can accomplish your strategy; then use the same criteria as for brand awareness campaigns to rank them.

This set of criteria will help you organize your ideas and rank them:

1. Does the idea deliver on the strategy?

2. How likely is the audience to respond to this idea compared to the others?

3. Does the company have the resources to implement this idea, either alone or with outside help?

4. Are there any roadblocks to this idea?

Flesh It Out

Take the top two or three ideas and map out project plans to make it happen. Include tactics that are directly related to your goal. For example, for a reputation management strategy, you would include such tactics as setting up a listening station and actively monitoring social media channels. If you're considering a brand aware-ness campaign, you would include things like, "create a series of content with tips for our target audience" or "create a humorous video poking fun at our industry." Think about the high-level tactic and then all the tasks necessary to make it happen.

Organize Your Plans

Once you've documented what you're trying to accomplish, you need a road map of how to get there. The strategy is the starting point, but the tactics and project plans are where the work happens. Don't take this part of the process lightly. A phenomenal strategy can fail miserably with inferior execution. In fact, the project plan is arguably *the* most important part of your strategy. Why? Because although implementation is where most mistakes are made, it's also where great ideas get wings. To organize your plans, consider creating the following documents.

12-Month High-Level Road Map

This document prioritizes your initiatives and their associated tactics over a 12-month period (see Figure 3.4). It also sets expectations for the level of work required, and it identifies the resources needed to make it a reality. Share this document with management teams and vendors who are involved in your projects because it provides a single-page glance at your plan over a year.

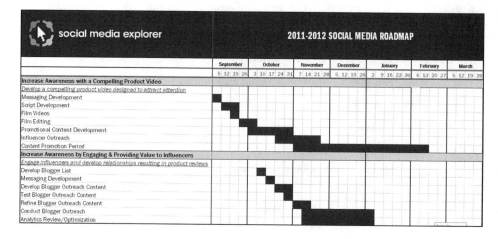

Figure 3.4   *The high-level road map provides an overview of the tactical plan for your strategy that fits on a single page.*

Tactical Project Plan

This document lays out all the tasks that need to be accomplished, the anticipated completion dates, and who is responsible for them (see Figure 3.5). It's typically completed for the upcoming quarter and adjusted each month.

social media explorer	2012 PROJECT PLAN			
Project Plan		Target Date	Responsible	Completion Date
January SME Tasks				
Select a Video Production Company				
Conduct a needs analysis with client				
Define client needs				
Create a list of potential vendors				
Interview vendors				
Review previous work from vendors				
Receive quotes				
Call references				
Finalize vendor selection				
Create Video				
Define project scope to receive vendor quotes				
Schedule filming dates				
Write script				
Review/edit script				
Finalize script/receive client approval				
Select talent for on-screen personality				
Prep talent				
Screen test with talent				
Film Video				
Video Edit				
Presentation of 1st draft to client				
Send feedback to vendor				
Receive final video				
January Client Tasks				
Create Video				
Create a list of internal talent for on-screen personalities				
Participate in screen test with talent				
Review 1st draft video and send feedback				
Approve final video				

Figure 3.5   *The project plan identifies all of the tasks that need to be completed to finish the projects on the road map.*

The next step is to figure out how you will actually measure your strategy's success. In the next chapter, you'll get an actionable measurement framework to illustrate its performance.

Hands-On Exercise: Prioritizing Brand Awareness Strategies

These worksheets are designed to help you through the brainstorming process and provide a framework for prioritizing your ideas.

Strategy Evaluation Matrix

In the following box, document your proposed strategy.

Proposed Strategy

In the next table, list the reasons why you think the idea is awesome. Then write all the things that could go wrong, limit success, or utterly kibosh the project. (These may be internal or external factors to the company.) Finally, rate the potential impact of your idea on the company on a scale of 1 to 5. 1 means very little impact and 5 means a tremendous impact. When you consider impact, remember to relate the impact to core business goals, increased sales volume, increased revenue, or decreased costs. Ultimately, you can determine the criteria to measure the potential impact. The only caveat is that you have to use the same criteria across all the strategies you're considering.

Pros	Cons	Potential Impact

Once you've gone through this exercise with each strategy idea, it's important to evaluate another set of criteria: feasibility. Some of the greatest ideas just aren't realistic for a company. You might have a fantastic idea for a Super Bowl commercial, but if you work for a start-up with limited resources, clearly your idea isn't feasible. Don't bite off more than you can chew. So in the table that follows, rate the level of resources required to execute the strategy. Move on to risk and consider the risks your strategy could create for the company. Could a mistake lead to a lawsuit? Then consider the potential impact the strategy could have for the company. Could this strategy have a huge impact on the brand image of the company with very little risk and level of effort?

You can't make decisions based on your company's aversion to risk, but you need to understand your own confidence levels and what types of risk you need to mitigate. If you have a high level of confidence, and you develop a plan to increase feasibility and mitigate risk, you will be prepared for your management team's questions. There may be other strategies that require little effort but that you feel have a substantially positive impact—you may move them to the top of the list when you scrutinize them using these same criteria.

Rate from 1 to 5. 1 = Least, 5 = Most			
Top Three Strategies	Level of Effort	Risk	Impact

## 4

Measuring Social Media for Brand Awareness

You have a good idea of the types of strategies you think will be effective at increasing awareness and positive perceptions for your company. That's fantastic, but the true test of a good strategy is how difficult it is to measure its impact on the company. Chapter 3, "Social Media for Brand Awareness," provided a framework for developing a measurable social media strategy, but now you need to look at what you're actually going to measure.

This book has discussed two types of brand awareness strategies: brand awareness campaigns and reputation management. The measurement approaches for these are different and should be considered separately. But a few core elements are important for both approaches.

The first step in defining your measurement approach is to understand that the metrics that are important to you and the metrics that are important to your management team are different. That said, they're equally important in their ability to prove and sustain your strategy.

Community Manager

These are metrics that help you determine whether you're moving the needle in the right direction. They give you an idea of which content is and isn't working, what you should do more of, and what you should stop doing. These are the metrics that you've likely heard the most about in social media measurement—things like fans, followers, and mentions.

Executive Management Team Metrics

Executive management metrics are different. They summarize key data points in a digestible form. These metrics are so simple that even the even executives who aren't well-versed in social media can understand them. Further, these metrics should have a history in the company so the executive has a realistic baseline for success. Does that sound impossible? You'll see exactly what these team metrics look like a little later.

> *Brand value is very much like an onion. It has layers and a core. The core is the user who will stick with you until the very end.*
>
> —Edwin Artzt

Translating Social Media for Executives

Too many marketers are trying to get their management team to understand what a retweet is, what a mention is, what a like is. Furthermore, they struggle to explain why such things matter to the company. Face it: It's going to take a while before your management team truly understands the metrics associated with social media channels. When the Web came around, did most executives really understand what a unique visitor versus a visit was? It took some time for executives to become familiar with the lingo and understand the benchmarks for success. It wouldn't be surprising if members of your management team still don't know the difference between unique visitors and visits. But that's absolutely okay. They don't need to understand the nitty-gritty details of every marketing channel. Instead, they need to understand how the marketing channels you're using contribute to the bottom line.

Social media measurement doesn't require executives to hold a Ph.D. in cool to understand it. We will focus on how you can translate social media into metrics that executives already understand.

> *Social media measurement shouldn't require executives to hold a Ph.D. in cool to understand.*

Social Media Is Just Another Channel

Social media isn't some "special" marketing channel that's unlike any other; it's just one channel in your marketing mix. Many companies still use TV, radio, direct mail, email marketing, and a slew of other channels to communicate their messages and drive their bottom lines. When you talk to your management team, drop the jargon and refer to social media as what it is—a marketing channel. Whether you're trying to get a strategy approved or presenting the results of your plan, if the conversation turns to "What is Twitter again?" you've lost. Focus on the channel as a whole, not its techy parts. Turn your conversation from "tweets and status updates" to "exposure, engagement, and conversion."

Don't Measure Social Media in a Silo

If you recognize that social media is just another marketing channel, you can see the danger in measuring it in isolation from other marketing channels. To demonstrate the value of social media while you're working to build your audience, you must have some benchmarks. The only way to do that effectively is to isolate those who interact with the social media channel from those who don't. Then compare core metrics through the entire funnel and across all marketing channels—so you know how good those people are as customers and how well they convert when compared with other marketing channels. This requires campaign tracking to be integrated into your customer relationship management tool; that will let you measure through the life cycle of the customer. In Chapter 9, "Breaking Down the Barriers to Social Media Measurement," you'll see tips on how to get around the barriers to making this happen.

The Goal of Brand Awareness Campaigns

Brand awareness campaigns are designed to get your brand in front of new people and increase their recall of your brand name. The result should be a group of loyal followers excited about what your company does—so much so that they will consider your company if they need your product or service. At its core, brand awareness campaigns are measured by their ability to increase exposure, increase engagement, and drive conversions.

Complementary Marketing Channels

To ensure you aren't measuring social media in a silo, you need to understand which marketing channels have similarities that you can leverage for cross-functional measurement. Think about the marketing channels that are designed to raise awareness and change perception. The list falls into two channels: public relations and advertising.

The following marketing channels have common brand awareness objectives:

- Public relations
- Online advertising
- TV advertising
- Radio advertising
- Print advertising

The beauty is that because there are complementary channels with a long history in your company, you can leverage the data from those channels as benchmarks for success. Next is translating public relations and social media metrics into metrics that executives understand but that are agnostic to any specific marketing channel. The following table breaks this down.

Public Relations Metrics	Social Media Metrics	Channel-Agnostic Metric
Circulation	Fans/followers	Impressions
Pass along	Mentions, retweets, likes, shares	Engagements
Tone	Sentiment	Sentiment
Share of voice	Share of voice	Share of voice
Referral site traffic	Referral site traffic	Site visits
Conversions	Conversions	Conversions

Two fairly common public relations metrics were intentionally omitted from this table: ad equivalency and brand recall. First, ad equivalency or value was omitted because it can provide a false sense of achievement for public relations that doesn't relate to the core objective. Plus, that metric can't be measured accurately across the social media channel. How would you calculate the ad value of a tweet that may be present in someone's stream for a few seconds? The public relations software Cision measures a publicity value for the social channel, but its methodology is not clear, which can make it difficult to validate the results. Second, brand recall was not mentioned because the ability to accurately measure recall makes existing data questionable. Most measures of brand recall are found by doing surveys and focus groups, which are unrealistic for many marketers who are trying to show the value of social media.

The same process can be used to create agnostic measurements for online and offline advertising.

Online/Offline Advertising Metrics	Social Media Metrics	Channel Agnostic Metric
Ad impressions	Fans/followers	Impressions
Reach	Networks of fans/followers	Total reach
Click-through/CTR/site visits	Referral site traffic	Site visits
Conversions	Conversions	Conversions

This leaves a core set of metrics that can be used across all channels to measure brand awareness:

- Impressions
- Total reach
- Engagement
- Site visits
- Conversions
- Share of voice

The Goal of Reputation Management

Reputation management is about protecting your brand's reputation and increasing positive sentiment about your brand. The results should be a positive image for your company and the ability to quickly mitigate a crisis in a way that helps your company look responsive and honest. Reputation management is measured in terms of your ability to get the right message out, the time it takes you to respond to a crisis, and the sentiment people have about your brand in the wake of the crisis.

Reputation management is a grossly undermeasured area of marketing that has no established standard measurement. However, you can use a few core metrics to measure your progress.

Online Reputation Metrics
% Positive mentions
% Negative mentions
# of negative listings in the top 10 search engine results for target key words
Share of voice
Average time to respond to complaints

This provides you with a general framework for the metrics that are important to collect. The next step is to translate them into something that executive teams care about. Chapter 3 reviewed the following list of metrics for the exposure and influence category.

Exposure Metrics			
Twitter	Facebook	YouTube	LinkedIn
Impressions from content	Total reach	Channel views	Displayed in search results

Influence Metrics					
Calculated from the Networks of Influencers Who Mention the Brand Only on the Networks the Brand Was Mentioned					
Blog	Twitter	Facebook	Google+	YouTube	LinkedIn
RSS subscribers	Followers	Fans	Followers	Channel subscribers	Connections
Average monthly site traffic	Followers of those who retweet post	Friends of those who engage	Followers of those who +1		

All these metrics can be summarized into one measurement for your management team: *cost per impression*. Remember, for executives it is all about three things: sales volume, revenue, and cost. The one thing you can absolutely measure right now is cost, so use it to your advantage and start presenting your exposure and influence metrics as the cost per impression.

To calculate the cost per impression, simply add the data from the previous table to get one number called *impressions*. Then divide the budget assigned to social media or to your brand awareness campaign by the total number of impressions.

Calculating Cost per Impression

Social media budget / sum of total impressions that came
from the social channel = social media cost per impression

Impressions are pretty much a fluff metric. They hold little value because they represent the number of people who had the "potential" to see your brand, but probably didn't. However, impressions have a history as a metric, have a standard baseline for success, and continue to be calculated by companies. Therefore, although impressions are not one of my favorite metrics, they're used as a top-line measure of success in achieving exposure and influence.

The next area of metrics we'll review focus around engagement. The list of engagement metrics is impressive; there are many options to engage on social channels.

Engagement Metrics					
Blog	**Twitter**	**Facebook**	**Google+**	**YouTube**	**LinkedIn**
RSS subscribers	Followers	Fans	Followers	Subscribers	Company followers
New email subscribers	@ replies mentions	Engaged users	+1 on content	Channel views	Shares
Comments	Direct messages	Page stories	Comments	Video views	Group members
Comment likes	Retweets	People talking about this	Mentions	Comments	Group discussions
Email to a friend	Brand-related hashtag mentions	Check-ins	Shares	Clicks on links shared	Clicks on links shared
Bookmark	Clicks on links shared	Clicks on links shared	Clicks on links shared	Site visits	Site visits
	Site visits	Site visits	Site visits		

How do you distill that into a metric that executives care about? It's tougher because there isn't a true standard to use. But there *is* a metric that requires little explanation: *cost per engagement*. Because *engagement* is defined as users who took physical action to interact with the brand, it immediately demonstrates value.

To calculate the cost per engagement, simply add the data from the previous table into one number called engagements. Then divide the total budget assigned to social media or to your brand awareness campaign by the total number of engagements.

Calculating Cost per Engagement

Social media budget / sum of total engagements in
the social channel = social media cost per engagement

Finally, it's important to measure all the way through the funnel. If your goal is
to generate brand awareness or protect your brand's reputation, and you do your
job well, sales will result. So you still need to measure how your actions affected
conversions.

The core metric at the bottom of the funnel is conversions. *Conversions* are singular actions a user can take. They are not a "conversion into a fan" or any other type
of fluff metric that can't drive revenue to the company. There are two such types
of conversions. The first involves someone who has provided contact information
that you can use for future marketing purposes, which means it has to include
an opt-in to your email marketing programs. The second involves someone who
actually bought something. That's it. Conversions have gotten a tainted reputation
because some marketers use the term to disguise non-revenue-generating actions.
Don't be that marketer. Be the one who understands the bottom line.

Soft Conversion	Hard Conversion
Action taken by someone who has provided contact information and opted in to receive future marketing materials	Action taken by someone who has provided contact information to indicate interest in your products and services or someone who has made a purchase

Calculating Cost per Conversion

Social media budget / sum of total conversions from
the social channel = social media cost per conversion

To calculate the cost per conversion, simply add all of the conversions from the
social channel. Then, divide the budget assigned to social media or to your brand
awareness campaign by the total number of conversions.

Handling Salaries in Cost Metrics

A common question is how to handle salaries when you're presenting social media
using cost metrics. Be consistent. If you include salaries in reports for your
pay-per-click campaign, TV advertising, PR, and direct mail channels, then add
them into your measurement approach so you're consistent. However, if you don't
figure salaries into those reports, it doesn't make sense to include them in the
social media reports. That would eliminate your ability to compare apples to apples

across marketing channels. It's a challenge because the resources it takes to manage your presence are a large social media expense. However, that battle is worth fighting. If you're required to add salaries into your social media reports, adjust all the other marketing reports to include salaries as well. The key issue is whether the marketing channels are being measured consistently so that the metrics are truly comparable. Stand up for measurement equality across all marketing teams.

Hands-On Exercise: Aligning Social Media Metrics to Metrics That Matter

The following worksheets are designed to help you align the metrics you're presenting for social media with core business metrics. Fill in the metrics you currently use to evaluate success. Then think about why that metric matters. When you present it, what are you attempting to demonstrate to your management team? Then identify whether the metric can be translated into a derivative of sales volume, revenue, or cost. Finally, identify the core business metric you will use in the future. You will likely have several metrics with the same resulting business metric. That is exactly what you should end up with. In the next exercise, you will reconcile those metrics. Remember, the three cost metrics are cost per impression, cost per engagement, and cost per conversion or cost per lead. Sales volume is the measure of units or hours sold, typically calculated as average sales volume per customer, while revenue is typically calculated as average revenue per customer. Although you also will show the total number of units sold and the total revenue, these calculations will allow you to demonstrate how profitable your customers are. For now, don't worry about how you will get the data. All that will come together before the end of the book.

Social Media Metric	Demonstrates	Aligns Best With	Business Metric
Fans	Reach	Sales volume	Cost per impression
		Revenue	
		Cost	
		Sales volume	
		Revenue	
		Cost	
		Sales volume	
		Revenue	
		Cost	

Social Media Metric	Demonstrates	Aligns Best With	Business Metric
		Sales volume Revenue Cost	
		Sales volume Revenue Cost	
		Sales volume Revenue Cost	
		Sales volume Revenue Cost	
		Sales volume Revenue Cost	
		Sales volume Revenue Cost	
		Sales volume Revenue Cost	
		Sales volume Revenue Cost	
		Sales volume Revenue Cost	

You likely have a list of several metrics that will be measured with the same business metric. Hopefully, you feel a weight lifting off your shoulders because now you have a group of social metrics that can be distilled into a few business metrics that your management team will understand. In the following table, group all the metrics with like business metrics so you have a list that you can use to create your next report. After you have the list of everything that will be measured in cost per impression, for example, you will group all those metrics together in your reporting and present one overall cost per impression to your management team.

Social Media Metric	Business Metric

5

Social Media for Lead Generation

When you hear the words lead generation in the same sentence as social media, how does it make you feel? For many it calls up slimy salespeople broadcasting status updates begging people to buy their products or services. Everyone has quickly unfollowed, unfriended, or even blocked users who do this. That's not what this chapter is going to be about. Perspective has shifted about social media lead generation, and people are beginning to see that they're creating something valuable that, when handled the right way, can generate business for their company. They recognize the delicate balance between providing value and generating sales interest from followers. If you are doing your job well in social media, sales will result. The big question is, can you track them and attribute them to your social media efforts?

First, it's important to understand how leads can be generated through social media. You may find that a prospective buyer tweets your corporate account asking questions about your product or service, creating a direct lead from Twitter. Another option is that a prospect could click on a link to your blog from an article you promoted. Once on your blog, the prospect could take actions like subscribing to your blog or even filling out a lead generation form. These are both leads that came directly from the social channel and are considered direct social media leads. There are also leads who interact with your social media channels but actually become a lead through another marketing channel, such as pay-per-click advertising. In this case, social media is contributing to the sale, but this is an indirect social media lead. This is important to understand from a tracking perspective. Mainly because tracking an indirect social media lead can be more difficult, but it could be a large portion of the leads you are generating. Ultimately, for this chapter a lead is defined as a prospect who has provided their contact information as a result of a call to action. This can be a result of a direct social media activity, or it could be the result of social media participating in the process of traditional marketing activities.

Where Lead Generation Fits into the Funnel

Lead generation is the last stage in the funnel before the big payoff—money! Envision big piles of money sitting underneath your sales funnel. Then ask: How much did your strategy contribute to that pile—one bill? Or thousands? If you know you delivered a healthy percentage of that pile, you should jump up and down and roll around in all that money!

But if not, you need to get serious about whether your social media strategy is delivering all it can. Whatever your social media goal, your efforts should put more opportunities in the top of the funnel. If handled properly, they will result in additional revenue. This is a crucial piece of your social media strategy—it is where you will finally demonstrate actual financial return for your organization.

Understanding Social Media Lead Generation

Lead generation in social media relies on your ability to add value for your prospects and effectively drive interest for your products or services. This is best done with a strategy that delivers content that not only is interesting to your potential customers, but drives them through the sales funnel.

AmeriFirst Home Mortgage is a great example of how to drive sales with content. Mortgage companies are probably high on your "spammy marketers" list. You've gotten endless mailings trumpeting lower rates if you just call them today. But AmeriFirst is different. It understands that people have questions about the mortgage process and are likely searching for answers no matter where they are in the loan process. In response, AmeriFirst provides a variety of resources, including these downloadable guides: "The Essential Guide to Buying Your First Home," "The Ultimate Guide to Home Improvement Loans," and "The Road to Mortgage Ready Credit" (see Figure 5.1).

Figure 5.1   *AmeriFirst uses content to drive decision making.*

These guides are clearly aligned with loan products AmeriFirst offers, but they are equally valuable for consumers who are going through the loan process or considering applying for a loan. The guides are refreshing because AmeriFirst doesn't beat you over the head to convert you into a client. Instead, it provides information. This approach helps AmeriFirst in several ways.

First, it helps attract leads through organic search. According to Dan Moyle, the certified inbound marketing specialist for AmeriFirst, "We can honestly say that we don't have to advertise anymore. We've tested other types of marketing like TV, radio, billboards, direct mail, and even pay-per-click campaigns. We've found that they are a waste of money in our space. Now we focus on driving online leads using a content marketing approach."

Second, it gives AmeriFirst something to offer to fans and followers. Moyle went on to say: "Talking about the home-buying process isn't a shout campaign. We focus on providing value to consumers who are purchasing a home. We answer common questions in videos and use our blog to share resources about the home-buying process, information about the housing market, and even home design tips. It's not all about us. We share information from third parties as often as we share information provided from our team."

Third, it allows AmeriFirst to optimize its results. "We've found that it isn't just a flash in the pan. We have seen consistent, month-over-month growth in the number of views and the number of leads generated for our mortgage consultants. And we've received feedback that the quality of the leads we are sending continues to get better over time."

Another thing AmeriFirst is doing right is collecting contact information from anyone who downloads the guides. The company then uses this information for email marketing campaigns that keep driving value and facilitating the sales process. That content drives potential clients through the sales funnel without pushing the sale.

What has this approach done for AmeriFirst's business? Its landing pages are achieving a 35% conversion rate, it has seen a 546% increase in traffic to its website, and its lead generation has skyrocketed by 1,316%.

Handling Social Media Leads

At its core, lead generation is about getting contact information from potential buyers. Once you have that contact information, you can deploy marketing campaigns to help the sales process along. However, the leads that come through social media may be at a different stage in the sales process, so it's important to be able to identify leads that touched social media from those who didn't.

You will generate two types of leads through social media efforts. Understanding the difference is crucial to your success.

Soft Leads

Soft leads are people who have provided contact information in exchange for a piece of content that doesn't indicate interest in your products or services. It's content that's relevant to the audience, but at this point the lead has only indicated an interest in your content. That's it. If you send the lead emails that scream, "Buy me! Buy me!" you will drive your unsubscribe rate through the roof. Quickly. In the business-to-business (B2B) marketing world (where there usually is a sales team that processes leads), you want to be careful about handing over these leads too early. They aren't ready for the sales process. Besides sending the leads heading for the hills, you'll also probably get guff from your sales team for sending them "unqualified" leads and wasting their time. And the turf war may begin. Sales teams: "The leads that marketing is sending us suck!" Marketing teams: "The sales team is incompetent; they can't convert these great leads!" If you're sending soft leads to the sales team, your leads *do* suck. They're valuable, but not for the sales team. Yet.

The type of content that would be considered a soft conversion varies greatly by industry.

Conversions coming from these HubSpot e-books would be considered soft leads:

100 Awesome Charts and Graphs

How to Use Pinterest for Business

Step-By-Step Guide to New Facebook Business Page Timelines

Do you see why? HubSpot sells SEO and marketing automation software. These e-books have nothing to do with the problem their software solves, but they're extremely helpful for their target audience: marketers. They provide value and demonstrate HubSpot's thought leadership for its audience. Still, the people who view this content should be treated differently from leads who indicate product interest.

Hard Leads

Hard leads are people who have provided contact information in a form that says they are interested in your products or services. Software companies may offer demonstrations or webinars about their products. People who fill out a lead generation form for these sessions would be hard leads because if they have signed up, they are likely interested in learning more about purchasing the software. Some content will indicate that people are researching solutions to a problem, whereas other types of content show them in the decision-making process. It is important to distinguish between the types because you should handle them differently.

Continuing with the HubSpot example, the content Hubspot produced that generates hard leads includes the following:

Researching Solutions to Problems HubSpot Solves

The Definitive Blueprint: Lead Management

Inbound Lead Generation Kit

SEO for Lead Generation Kit

Content That Indicates Purchase Intent for HubSpot

Free Trial

See the Software

Take the Feature Tour

Free Demo

Figure 5.2 shows calls to action that indicate product interest such as demonstrations and trials. A call to action that is related to the sales process helps to distinguish those who are closer to making a decision. This is important because other types of calls to action, such as Hubspot's e-book *100 Awesome Charts and Graphs*, relate more to informative content and are difficult to correlate to actual purchase intent.

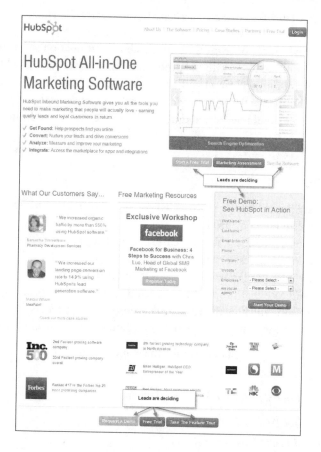

Figure 5.2   *Calls to action for demos, trials, and tours indicate the decision phase.*

Leads who are researching solutions are earlier in the buying process and can be sent email campaigns urging them to try a trial or demo, whereas those who have asked to see the product can be shunted into the active sales follow-up process. If you can accurately discern this difference, you can pass the right leads to your sales team. This will make you the rock star who delivers the leads that help your team hit monthly sales goals.

How to Kill the Sale

Have you attempted to qualify leads but found that your conversion rates are atrocious? Look at what you're sending them. A common mistake is to put leads who came from social channels in line to get your standard email marketing campaigns. In the business-to-consumer (B2C) space, that means your leads will suddenly get emails offering coupon after coupon, while in the B2B space they'll get overly promotional, hard-sell emails.

Those are the serial killers of social media leads. Those emails aren't aligned with the relationship you've built with your social media following. They were thinking you respected them, understood their needs, and wanted to provide value. Then bam, you're pushing them to buy something. That kind of perceived bait-and-switch will destroy the trust you worked so hard to build, and it will drive your social media leads straight to your competition.

Take a hard look at the emails your social media leads will receive. Audit them for tone, content, and relationship-nurturing potential. If your emails don't reflect the type of content you want your leads to receive, fix them—fast! If not, you could have just lost some customers.

Developing a Measurable Strategy for Lead Generation

Now that you understand more about social media lead generation, put that knowledge to work. Before you develop your strategy, figure out what tools you'll need to be successful. In social media, your lead generation tool is content. Think about the products or services you offer and ask yourself: How do new clients make decisions? What are common sales objections? Why do they select your competitors? Then think about what content you can produce that will encourage them to buy—and to buy from you.

Marketers produce three types of content: promotional content, informative content, and decision-making content.

Promotional Content

Promotional content is designed to raise awareness about a specific campaign. On social media, that largely means chatter about contests, special offers, discounts, and coming events. This content is important, but it can't be your only type of content, or your social channels will look like an advertising billboard. Companies wonder why they struggle to build audiences, but upon analysis you see that their social media presence consists of news releases, product information, and sales offers. They only talk about themselves. It's not surprising—that's what marketers have spent years learning how to do. Unfortunately, it just doesn't work in social media. Social media is designed for two-way conversations. So in addition to the crucial, traditional promotional content, your organization will have to dive into conversations with your audience and will have to share content from others.

Informative Content

Informative content is designed to provide value to your audience. It may have nothing to do with the products or services you provide, but it will help your target audience with common challenges or needs. Informative content doesn't have to be produced by your company; it can be a mix of information you provide and valuable resources you've found from others. Ideally, it includes a healthy measure of quality content from others and isn't just another stream of content from you. It is important to balance content about your company with valuable content for your audience. While many consider social media another broadcast channel for marketing messages, there is a better approach.

By providing informative content to your audience, you earn the right to talk about yourself. As a marketer whose job it is to broadcast messages about your company, earning the right to talk about yourself is an interesting perspective, isn't it? In more traditional marketing channels, you pay to play your commercial or radio spot, and for some reason there's a similar approach to social media channels. The reality is that the success of your social media channels is owned by your audience. To demonstrate success, you have to cater to their needs. They don't *need* to hear about you; they *choose* to hear about you. Social media is not a pay-to-play channel. By sharing relevant resources that provide tremendous value to your audience, they're likely to respond more favorably when you spend a little time talking about yourself.

What is a healthy mix of content about you? The Pareto Principle, or the 80-20 rule, is a good place to start. And no, that doesn't mean that 80% of your content is about you. Less than 20% of your content should be about you. Or, for every two posts you write promoting your own content on your social channels, you should have eight status updates promoting good content from someone else. The closer you can get to 90-10—or even 95-5—the better. You are sharing a tremendous amount of value that doesn't center around your company, and that informative content is very important to your success.

You may have certain types of high-value informational content that can be used to convert leads that are considered higher funnel leads, meaning they are earlier in the buying process. Informational content such as guides, e-books, and webinars should be placed behind a lead form because these are still valuable leads. However, it is important that you categorize leads coming from this content differently than you categorize leads coming from decision-making content as described in the next section. This will allow you to send email campaigns that are designed specifically for where the lead is in the buying process.

Decision-Making Content

The final category of content is decision-making content. Decision-making content is designed to help you through the decision-making process in selecting your product or service. It may contain information about common objections, outline decision-making criteria, and detail information that is important to understand when making a purchase. Marketers typically underutilize this type of content. While they're providing value and not being pushy, they sometimes forget that their job is to drive sales and that sales content doesn't have to be the next promotion or discount.

Decision-making content provides tremendous value to your target audience— while it tees up the opportunity to talk about your company. It also helps to identify when people are in the research and decision-making phase of the buying cycle. It's the holy grail of content.

If you don't have decision-making content in your arsenal, you're missing a tremendous opportunity to deliver qualified leads and sales to your company.

To figure out what type of decision-making content is relevant to your business, sit down with your sales department and ask what questions they get during the sales process. If you are a B2C company, think about what factors go into the decision to purchase your product. Then create a list of topics that helps answer those questions, or show how your product relates to common decision-making factors.

Place all decision-making content behind a lead generation form for B2B companies and an email signup form for B2C companies. People looking at this content are potential customers—if you don't collect their contact information, you won't have a way to send them valuable information that keeps you top of mind in the decision-making process. Some say that placing this type of content behind a form will cut the number of people who access the content. That may be true, but it also weeds out looky-loos. Do you want a group of people you can't contact who may or may not be serious buyers, or a list of people you can contact who are more likely to buy?

Finally, decision-making content tends to be the precursor to calls to action—like a product demonstration, free trial of your product, or online purchase. Think about it like an early indicator of product interest. If you could clearly distinguish between website visitors who had purchase intent from those just browsing, would you want that? Of course you would. You want to pay more attention to those who are serious and not waste effort on those who aren't.

Where Does Lead Scoring Fit?

The other benefit to categorizing your content into informative and decision-making content is that it allows you to utilize lead scoring models to better differentiate between qualified leads and those just browsing. In B2B marketing, lead scoring is an important part of delivering qualified leads in an effective lead generation strategy. This can also be leveraged in B2C companies, but the qualified leads wouldn't be forwarded to a sales team. They would be sent more sales-related email campaigns. For our purposes here, this will be illustrated with a B2B company.

Once you have your lead generation content strategy in full swing and social media is continuing to drive traffic, it is likely there will be a significant increase in online leads. This will require some organization to how leads are handled so the sales team doesn't become overwhelmed with leads that aren't ready to buy. A lead scoring methodology can help to segment leads and drive the appropriate follow-up process. The goal is to place leads into one of three categories:

Slow

Medium

Fast

Slow Leads

Slow leads are those that are least likely to close in a short amount of time. This will vary based upon your typical sales cycle from company to company, but it is typically representative of leads that haven't indicated product interest. You want to stay top of mind with these potential customers, but you don't want the sales team to spend a lot of day-to-day time trying to push them to the sale because they could be missing out on opportunities with leads that are in the decision-making phase. For these prospects, marketing typically provides top of mind content on a monthly basis in the form of a newsletter or another general monthly email.

Medium Leads

Medium leads are leads that are likely to buy at some point in the future, but they either aren't ready yet or they have indicated they will be making a decision down the road. These leads are still in the consideration phase and likely actively researching solutions. This window of time is the most likely time for a prospect to select a competitor. Medium leads tend to be people who have looked at a piece of decision-making content, but have yet to follow up on activities that would place them in the active sales process. With social media efforts, this can be a very large group of people that would be too resource-intensive for a hands-on effort sales from the sales team because they are focused on the leads that are ready to buy now. Therefore, these leads are a large focus for marketing teams. The goal is to provide content that will drive the prospect to the next phase in the funnel, such as additional decision-making content, top of mind content and opportunities to take the next step in the sales process.

Fast Leads

Fast leads are the prospects that have been placed into the active buying process. They are the leads that have indicated they are ready to buy and are making a decision. One way to identify leads that are fast leads is based upon whether their purchase has been added to the sales forecast. Many times there is concern over delaying the sale with these leads, so marketing may take a hands-off approach. The sales person has the most intimate knowledge of what is important to these prospects, so follow up is typically handled manually by the sales team.

Types of Lead Scoring Models

Categorizing leads into slow, medium and fast is just one option for lead scoring. There are several other models available include points-based lead scoring, activity-based lead scoring, and even manual lead scoring. Each of these models is discussed in detail in Chapter 6, "Measuring Social Media for Lead Generation." But at this point it's important to know that if you can develop a way to separate qualified leads from unqualified leads, your strategy will be far more successful.

Optimizing the Path to Conversion

Now that you understand the types of content you'll need and the basics for lead scoring, it's time to look at the path to conversion. The path to conversion represents the steps a potential buyer takes to buy your products or services. Many companies make this process extremely difficult and then wonder why their social media efforts aren't generating sales.

Envision your social media channels. If people wanted to buy your products or services from Twitter, what would they have to do? Twitter doesn't make that process easy for anyone. But what changes could you make to your bio or your website link to make it easier? Where do people land when they click the website link, your home page? What do they need to do from there to make a purchase?

What about Facebook? Do you make it super easy to buy (like Under Armour), or do you expect people to click on the About page and then click on your website to get to your home page to look for a way to buy?

Check this process for every social network you have a presence on. Each social media network is unique, so making it easy to buy will be different for each one, but you should do what you can on all of them.

One of the most overlooked social networks is your blog, and it's ripe for enhancing the path to conversion (see Figure 5.3).

Figure 5.3 *HubSpot illustrates a blog that has optimized the path to conversion.*

Where does your company publish its ongoing content? Your blog. When you post about this content on social networks, where do you send people? Your blog.

Blogs are the central hub for social media content, and they're a crucial element in your path to conversion. Blog posts should become your most optimized landing pages because a blog lets you post relevant content on the fly without a web developer. Plus, you can optimize those blog posts to drive organic search traffic from Google and Bing to deliver even more results. Don't ignore your blog's conversion potential or the amount of traffic you're sending there. If you haven't optimized your blog to be an easy path to conversion, you aren't alone. Sometimes even the industry professionals forget. Eloqua, a marketing automation provider, hasn't optimized the path to conversion from its blog, which is ironic considering the company's blog is called "It's All About Revenue" (see Figure 5.4).

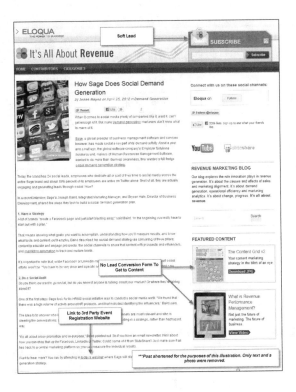

Figure 5.4   *Eloqua, a marketing automation provider, hasn't optimized its path to conversion.*

Defining Success Metrics

Before jumping into defining a lead generation strategy, define how you will measure success. Defining your success metrics early in the process will help you determine whether your strategy will produce your intended results. Lead generation metrics are easy to co-opt from other marketing channels. Remember, solid lead generation strategies will not only drive leads from the social channel; they also will increase organic leads from search engines because you're developing content for your audience that can be found in organic search. Therefore, you will include metrics that are related to *SEO*, or search engine optimization.

Conversion Metrics		
Online Advertising	SEO	Social Media
Cost per click	Cost per inbound link	Cost per click
Cost per site visit	Cost per organic site visit	Cost per site visit
Cost per conversion	Cost per conversion	Cost per conversion
Conversion rate	Conversion rate	Conversion rate
Cost per lead	Cost per lead	Cost per lead
Cost per sale	Cost per sale	Cost per sale
Revenue generated	Revenue generated	Revenue generated
Units sold	Units sold	Units sold
Revenue per customer	Revenue per customer	Revenue per customer
Profit per customer	Profit per customer	Profit per customer

There are only slight variations in how metrics are referenced within these three channels. This makes aligning metrics across channels in lead generation a lot easier than it was for brand awareness.

Define Your Strategy

At this point, you have the framework to develop a solid lead generation strategy. So go a little crazy and brainstorm how you can convert social media fans and followers into leads. Which channels are best positioned to drive leads? What conversion points are you driving toward?

Ask yourself the tough questions now because your management team is certainly going to. Lead generation is one thing that most executives understand. They think about it every day, and they work through the management team to find ways to get better at it because, at the end of the day, companies live and die according to what goes in and what comes out of the sales funnel. If you've ever been laid off from a company, you understand how important leads are to the bottom line.

While you're brainstorming, think about where you can add value in the lead generation process. Can you help bring down the costs of generating leads? Every dollar you save the company in customer acquisition costs will go straight to the bottom line. Can you improve conversion rates? If you show that social media converts leads at a higher rate than other marketing channels do, your colleagues will take notice. Can you provide decision-making content that you can test in pay-per-click advertising campaigns, in addition to the social media outreach you're planning? Everything isn't about proving that social media is better than other marketing channels. One of the most effective strategies you can deploy is to show how decision-making content can help other marketing channels deliver results.

Example Strategy A:

Increase lead conversions from the corporate blog

Example Strategy B:

Optimize the path to conversion from third-party social networks

Example Strategy C:

Develop and promote content to facilitate prospects' decision-making process

Example Strategy D:

Develop an integrated communications plan for lead conversion from social media channels

There is an important thing to be aware of when you're developing lead generation strategies for social media: Social media is great at bringing leads to the door. But those leads tend to convert into new customers through other marketing channels like organic search, pay-per-click advertising, and email marketing. That's why it's so important to look at what you have going on in those other channels to make sure it will nurture the social media leads and not slam the door on sales. With recent developments like Google Analytics' social reporting feature, you can get a better understanding of where social media contributes through the entire conversion process.

In basketball, two stats are relevant to this analogy: points and assists. Points define whether the team wins or loses, and in the marketing world, points are conversions. Assists are when a player makes a pass that enables a teammate to score. Often that player does a tremendous amount of work to get the ball down court— he dodges, cuts, and spins around defenders. When he is almost to the basket, he makes a quick pass to his teammate, who takes it to the hoop for a crowd-pleasing slam dunk.

Social media is the almighty assist in lead generation strategies. Sometimes social media can bring a lead to the table and close the deal. But in most cases, social media does a lot of legwork to bring the lead to the table and then passes it to another marketing channel equipped to drive it to conversion. So while you're brainstorming your strategies, consider which marketing channels increase social media conversions. Where would social media leads go once they are ready to buy? Would they come straight to your website? Would they do a Google search for your company? Will they forget your company name and do a search for the type of product or service you provide and click on your site once they are reminded of your company? Whatever the path to conversion looks like, make sure your strategy facilitates it all along the way.

Define How You Will Do It

When you have your strategies defined, consider how you'll accomplish them. Think about their budgetary, staff, content, and cross-team needs. Do you have the

> *Social media is the almighty assist in lead generation strategies.*

resources to be successful? If not, what more do you need? Does your team have the capacity to implement the strategy, or will you need to outsource parts of it? These considerations may determine how realistic the strategy is for you and your resources.

Then think about the content you'll need to develop for promotional purposes, for informative or educational purposes, and for decision-making purposes. Which type of content will facilitate the sales process? What do you need to change about your content production? What can you do to optimize the path to conversion? Then consider which of these will have the biggest effect with the least amount of effort. These are good places to start for short-term wins.

Flesh It Out

After you have a better framework for your strategies and the necessary resources, flesh out the ideas. Prioritize the efforts and map out the time required for implementation. What will you need to do to get the approvals you need? Who are your decision makers?

Develop a mini-action plan for what's left to be accomplished before moving forward.

Organize Your Plans

Approval can come down to how strong your action plans are, so prepare as much as you can. Break a big strategy into palatable pieces so it doesn't overwhelm your executive team. To that end, organize your planning documents into a prioritized list of initiatives, a high-level overview, and a draft of your implementation schedule framework. (The same documents that were recommended for a brand awareness strategy are important here.)

12-Month High-Level Road Map

This document prioritizes your initiatives and their correlating tactics over a 12-month period (see Figure 5.5). It also sets expectations for the level of work required, and it identifies the resources needed to make it a reality. This concise, one-page document is great to share with management teams and outside vendors who are involved in your projects. If needed, it can identify budgets for each initiative, broken down by expense categories.

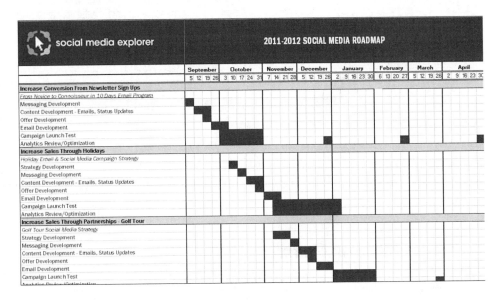

Figure 5.5 *The 12-month roadmap provides a quick overview of your strategy.*

Tactical Project Plan

The tactical plan is a project plan (see Figure 5.6). It lays out the tasks to be accomplished, the anticipated completion dates, and the personnel responsible for them. It's typically completed for an upcoming quarter and adjusted based on monthly progress.

Hands-On Exercise: Prioritizing Lead Generation Strategies

Just as you did with brand awareness strategies, you need to prioritize your lead generation strategies. These worksheets will help you go through the brainstorming process and provide a framework for prioritizing your ideas.

social media explorer 2012 PROJECT PLAN			
Project Plan	**Target Date**	**Responsible**	**Completion Date**
January SME Tasks			
Blog Conversion Optimization Project			
Develop Wireframes			
Get Wireframe Approval			
Develop Design Comps			
Send Feedback on Design Comps			
Get Approval on Design Comps			
Implement Design Comps			
Site Testing			
Web Form Testing			
Confirm Web Forms Populate Correct Lists in Email System			
Changes Deployed to Live Site			
Decision Making Content Production			
Work with client to develop prioritized list of decision making content topics			
Provide outline of Phase I e-book content to writers			
Draft of Phase I e-books review with client			
Feedback on Phase I e-book content to writers			
Finalize Phase I e-book content delivered to client for implementation on landing page			
e-book call to action designs delivered to client for implementation on blog			
January Client Tasks			
Blog Conversion Optimization Project			
Send Feedback on Must-Haves for Wire Frames			
Review and Approve Wire Frames			
Review and Send Feedback on Design Comps			
Approve Design Comps			
Conduct Website Testing with SME			
Confirm Web Deployment Approval			

Figure 5.6   *The project plan outlines the projects and their associated tasks.*

Strategy Evaluation Matrix

In the box, document your proposed strategy.

Proposed Strategy

In the next table, list the reasons you think the idea is awesome. Then write down all the things that could go wrong, hold back success, or kibosh the project. (These may be internal or external factors.) Finally, rate the potential impact of your idea on the company on a scale of 1 to 5. 1 means very little impact, and 5 means a tremendous impact. When you consider impact, remember to relate the impact to core business goals, increased sales volume, increased revenue, or decreased costs. Ultimately, you can determine the criteria to measure the potential impact, but remember that you have to use the same criteria across all the strategies you're considering.

Pros	Cons	Potential Impact

Once you've gone through this exercise with each strategy idea, it's important to evaluate feasibility. If implementing a marketing automation system will help you better define leads, but would require a 12-month implementation process for your company, it shouldn't be at the top of your list. In the table that follows, rate the level of resources required to execute the strategy. Move on to risk, and consider the risks your strategy could create for the company. Could a mistake in lead qualification cause your company to lose a lot of revenue downstream? If so, ensuring the lead qualification process isn't a manual process could be really important. Could your strategy potentially delay the sale for leads coming to the site from other marketing channels? Once you've evaluated risk, consider the impact the strategy could have for the company. Could this strategy have a huge impact on the number of quality leads generated for the company with a large upside, manageable risk and a low level of effort? Will it extend your sales funnel and provide a pool of leads that are earlier in the buying process but ripe for top of mind campaigns? Your goal is to ensure that when website visitors come from social media, there are multiple opportunities to convert into a lead that indicates where they are in the buying process. Do your strategies support the goal?

Rate from 1 to 5. 1 = Least, 5 = Most			
Top Three Strategies	Level of Effort	Risk	Impact

6

Measuring Social Media for Lead Generation

After you've prioritized your strategies, you can detail how you will measure success. You want to be able to measure any lead that has interacted with the social media channel, whether they came directly through social or they touched social media throughout the conversion process. For the sake of simplicity, we'll call a lead that has interacted with your social media channels somewhere in the sales process a social media lead. Chapter 9, "Breaking Down the Barriers to Social Media Measurement," will discuss the challenges with accurately tracking social media as a lead source, but for now we focus on leads who came from a social media channel prior to converting on your website. This is considered a last touch attribution model, meaning the lead source is defined as the marketing campaign the prospect touched last. Social media leads will perform differently from those in your other marketing channels. This doesn't make them less valuable—you're reaching them earlier in the sales cycle and beating your competition. Once you realize you're starting from an earlier point in the sales cycle, it makes sense that these leads probably will take longer to close. Set that expectation with your management team early, or they may write social media leads off as too slow to convert. If they write them off too early, you won't be able to show them how social media can outperform other marketing channels in priming the funnel for future sales. To show this potential, you need to measure lead generation activities a little differently, which will require structured lead management.

Measuring lead generation activities can be as simple as calculating how many leads were generated and how many convert, but that won't help you make better decisions about how you're treating leads. For lead generation strategies to work, your measurement approach should be able to accurately identify where a lead is in the buying cycle and focus on measuring your ability to move those leads to close.

> *The key is not to call the decision maker. The key is to have the decision maker call you.*
> —Jeffrey Gitomer

Identifying Lead Potential

An important element of your measurement approach is being able to identify where leads are in the funnel and understanding whether they're "qualified" to send to the sales team. Traditionally, businesses define qualified leads as individuals who have indicated interest in your product or service and provided enough information to facilitate follow up. Because not all social media leads are created equal, you need to identify leads that are sales ready and leads that need more nurturing. You have two options for measuring lead potential. First, you can use the system discussed earlier and identify whether the lead is a soft lead or a hard lead. That may be the best place to start because it's simple and easy to position with your management team. You can send soft leads one set of communications and hard leads a different set of communications to work on converting them.

The second option is to align with the current lead management system that is already in place. If the current lead management system doesn't account for how early social media leads are in the sales cycle, you can use several ways to tag leads and identify where they are in the funnel.

Organizations have different ways of identifying where leads are in the funnel. A simple way is to classify leads as slowest, slow, medium, fast and closed as shown in Figure 6.1—referring to how long it will take for the lead to convert into a sale. Slow leads take the longest time, whereas fast leads convert in the shortest time.

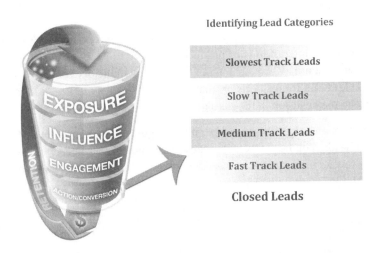

Figure 6.1 *Leads can be categorized into slowest, slow, medium, fast and closed to align with the sales funnel.*

Slowest Leads

The slowest group of leads may be those who have subscribed to the blog or an email newsletter. They're technically leads because they've provided contact information; however, they haven't really indicated interest in your products or services. You should send them your blog content and a monthly newsletter to stay top of mind until they do something that indicates their interest level has changed. Measuring this category really depends on how complex your sales process is. For some companies, this category may be unnecessary. However, if your company has a sales cycle that is 18 months or longer, you may want to consider separating this group.

Slow Leads

Slow leads are focused on information. They provided their contact information to get a piece of content that wasn't decision-making content. They appreciate what you send that helps them do their job better, and they may have looked at some decision-making content, but they haven't taken the next step. Nurture these leads. Provide them valuable content and offer a call to action to encourage them to move to the next stage in the sales process.

Medium Leads

Medium leads have provided their contact information for decision-making content; that indicates interest in your product and intent to purchase. They are leads that your sales team may be reaching out to for an introductory conversation. Offer these leads additional decision-making content with a call to action to purchase or take the next step in the sales process.

You should spend a significant amount of time figuring out how to convert this category of leads. You need to nurture these leads, but you also need to offer them the ability to take the next step in the sales process. Mastering conversion from this category of leads is your top priority.

Fast Leads

These are leads that the sales team has identified as great prospects who are ready to buy, and soon. They have been added to the forecast, and the sales team is actively working the lead. In business-to-business (B2B) companies, marketing will typically take a hands-off approach with these leads so there is no chance of interfering with a sale. You can use the same model for business-to-consumer (B2C) companies. The big difference is that instead of having a salesperson follow up, you have additional marketing communications working to drive the lead to sale. It will also change how much focus you put on driving conversions from the fast lead category. In B2C companies, the fast leads offer the greatest short-term revenue potential. The communications could be coupons and discounts or focus on your latest campaign. Therefore, as a B2C, you likely will put these leads as your top priority for conversion, whereas marketers for B2B companies will focus their efforts on medium leads.

Closed Leads

Closed leads are leads who have made a purchase. They have exited the active sales process and have entered into the customer retention process. Closed leads represent the sales that have been generated and are usually associated with a revenue value for the company. Identifying closed leads is an important step because it will help you determine lead close rates and evaluate their performance as customers.

Lead Scoring

When you have your lead generation content strategy in full swing and social media is continuing to drive traffic, it is likely there will be a significant increase in online leads. This will require some organization to how leads are handled so the sales team doesn't become overwhelmed with leads that aren't ready to buy. A lead scoring methodology can help to segment leads and drive the appropriate follow-up process. It will also help you measure how many leads touched the social media channel and where they are in the sales process. A higher lead score indicates how much interest the lead has shown and the likelihood of a sale. Lead scoring models provide a much deeper level of insight into what actions your leads are taking, and they help you choose the right time to communicate. Lead scoring can get complex but technology is making this easier. Marketing automation providers like Hubspot, Eloqua, Paradot, and Marketo provide lead scoring models that can be integrated with customer relationship management (CRM) systems like Salesforce to identify lead quality and the source of the lead. The integration with a CRM system is important because it will allow you to attach the number of leads with the amount of revenue that has been generated, while identifying the source of the lead. There are four types of lead scoring methodologies worth considering.

Types of Lead Scoring Models

There are many types of lead scoring models that can be implemented. The most important factor is that the marketing team can easily pull a list of prospects at each stage in the process in order to send the correct email marketing campaign.

Points-Based Lead Scoring

Some companies select a lead scoring model that assigns "points" to prospects based on their website activity and conversations with a sales person. Points ranges are used to determine where they are in the sales funnel and this triggers the appropriate follow-up marketing campaign. Many times a prospect will receive a certain number of points for visiting your website, such as 1 point per page, 5 points for product pages, 10 points for subscribing, and 20 points for filling out a lead generation form. One challenge to this type of scoring model is that someone can reach the range of a high-value lead through multiple visits to the website and the sales person who follows up identifies that the prospect is not actually at the point in the sales process their point score indicates. In the preceding example, by visiting blog content on a regular basis a prospect could accumulate 20 points and never have indicated product interest. This is typically handled through a manual adjustment of the point value for the prospect by the sales person to place them in the correct lead category. This means it is important to align the items that trigger an increase in the points assigned to the individual based upon true indications of product interest.

Activity-Based Lead Scoring

An off-shoot of points-based lead scoring is an activity-based lead scoring model. In this type of model the actions a prospect takes places them at different points in the sales funnel. This type of model is nice because it isn't possible to accumulate a high score by performing actions that aren't related to the product. Marketing automation systems such as Hubspot, Paradot, Eloqua make automated tracking of this information a reality. These systems monitor website activity, and when a visitor takes specific actions that are deemed to qualify them as a good prospect, they are placed in different automated follow-up processes. For example, if a prospect has filled out a lead generation form and attended a product demonstration, she may be marked as a fast lead. This type of model is much better at identifying true prospects and providing the opportunity for manual and automated follow-up.

Manual Lead Scoring

When technology costs are an issue, many small companies use a manual lead scoring model that is handled by the sales team. Typically this involves some kind of a score card that is evaluated during the first prospect meeting and is updated throughout the sales process. This can be effective for a small company but doesn't have the benefit of scale as the company grows. Further, it is solely reliant on the sales person keeping the lead score updated, which rarely happens as diligently as it should. Because the lead score determines the marketing follow-up that is used, it is risky to rely on a manual system, as the marketing team places a lot of value into the score that may or may not be updated. It's very possible that a sales person could be actively working with a client and forget to update the lead score. Because their lead score hasn't been updated, the marketing team could send an email communication that invites the prospect to a product demonstration from their sales person. This would be awkward at this stage, as the prospect has already seen a product demonstration and is ready to sign a contract.

Hybrid Lead Scoring

The most common lead scoring model is a hybrid model that allows for sales person input but doesn't rely on it. The lead score is updated based on website activities through a marketing automation system, which is passed to the CRM system. When a sales person is working with a prospect the lead score is updated based upon the lead status within the contact record. This disconnects the sales person from the lead scoring process and utilizes the natural flow through the sales process to place leads into the right categories. This creates a far more balanced approach to tracking online and offline activities without requiring a lot of manual input by the sales team.

Lead scoring isn't a requirement for a lead generation strategy, but it does make a big difference in your ability to ensure you are sending the right content to the right prospect at the right time. Ultimately, that will help you deliver better results.

It's Okay to Keep It Simple

If these systems are too complicated for your taste, you can break your leads into two categories: soft and hard. For soft leads, you will send campaigns designed to keep your company top of mind. You will offer calls to action that indicate whether the leads have product interest. For hard leads, you will send campaigns that are designed to drive the next stage in the sales process.

Whatever method you select, it's crucial that you identify where the leads you generate fit into the sales process. Then you need to measure how the leads perform.

Chapter 5, "Social Media for Lead Generation," reviewed the following list of conversion metrics. These metrics provide a framework for the metrics you will collect to monitor the progress of your strategy. Now you need to distill these metrics into a framework designed for your management team.

Social Media Manager Conversion Metrics		
Online Advertising	**SEO**	**Social Media**
Cost per click	Cost per inbound link	Cost per click
Cost per site visit	Cost per organic site visit	Cost per site visit
Cost per conversion	Cost per conversion	Cost per conversion
Conversion rate	Conversion rate	Conversion rate
Cost per lead	Cost per lead	Cost per lead
Cost per sale	Cost per sale	Cost per sale
Revenue generated	Revenue generated	Revenue generated
Units sold	Units sold	Units sold
Revenue per customer	Revenue per customer	Revenue per customer
Profit per customer	Profit per customer	Profit per customer

You will want to have a view of the data that allows you to get top-line numbers for each channel so that you can figure out how each social media channel is performing and adjust your strategies accordingly. Compare time periods to see whether leads are getting stuck in one of the lead categories. If few medium leads are moving forward to the fast stage each month, you might want to adjust your communications to see whether you can drive more leads into the fast category.

Social Media Manager Conversion Metrics			
Metric	Twitter	Facebook	Blog
# of slowest leads			
# of slow leads			
# of medium leads			
# of fast leads			
Conversion rate			
Cost per lead			
Cost per sale			
Revenue generated			
Units sold			
Revenue per customer			
Profit per customer			

These dashboards provide you with the data to evaluate your progress and optimize your results. From an analysis standpoint, a Twitter lead is a lead that came from Twitter and converted on your site, whereas a Facebook lead came from Facebook. This is where you are analyzing the social media channels that were the last point of interaction prior to the conversion. The next few dashboards are designed to roll this information into the metrics that matter to your management team. The first dashboard evaluates how social media is performing compared to other channels. This is important because it allows you to show improvements in conversion rates from one channel to the next. It also allows you to show decreases in cost for each category from one channel to the next. While you're getting started with lead generation efforts, it's likely that the number of leads you're generating will be small compared to those in the more established marketing channels. If you only generated 20 leads with social media, you might be almost embarrassed to present your results. But what if you show that you converted 10 of them into sales? A 50% conversion rate is impressive. And what if you show that they cost 70% less than other marketing channels? Don't sell yourself short by showing social media results in a silo.

Management Team Cross-Functional Conversion Metrics			
	Social Media	Online Advertising	SEO
# of leads generated			
Cost per lead			
Conversion rate			
Cost per sale			
Revenue generated			
Units sold			
Revenue per customer			
Profit per customer			

The second dashboard allows the management team to dig a little deeper into the social media metrics, while still providing a high-level overview.

Management Team Conversion Metrics			
	Slow Leads	Medium Leads	Fast Leads
# of leads generated			
Cost per lead			
Conversion rate			
Cost per sale			
Revenue generated			
Units sold			
Revenue per customer			
Profit per customer			

You're probably asking the same question that all marketers ask: How in the world am I going to connect a tweet to a sale? That, frankly, is the holy grail of social media measurement. If you could connect your results to revenue, you could answer the big return on investment (ROI) question. But the answer depends on several factors.

The first factor is your CRM system and whether it's connected to your web analytics package. If it is, you're in luck. With a few minor tweaks in how you publish content, you can pass the right data into the CRM system to pull reports. If it isn't connected, you have to accept that you can't get to revenue right now. You can, however, get to cost. You know how much you're spending. And if you are using Google Analytics on your website, you can track all the way through conversion of a lead. This book touches on the nitty-gritty of that later, but rest assured—there's a way to get the data you need.

Hands-On Exercise: Aligning Social Media Leads to the Sales Funnel

The metrics for measuring lead generation are fairly straightforward, and you saw how to break down the metrics. This exercise dives a little deeper into categorizing your leads. Several ways to identify lead categories were described in the previous chapter; this exercise is designed to help establish how you will identify lead categories for your organization.

Use Figure 6.2 to categorize your leads. Start at the bottom and name the lead category you send directly to the sales team. Then move up and create categories for leads that need a high level of nurturing to drive them to the next stage. Decide whether you want to break these into two categories. If you do, use the two spaces provided. If you don't, you will use one space and have an empty block at the top of the funnel. In the next category up the funnel, name the category of leads that have provided contact information but have not expressed interest in your products or services.

Hands-On Exercise: Aligning Marketing Lists to Lead Categories

The next area to look at is which web forms are used to generate leads and whether they align with the right marketing lists to receive the appropriate communications.

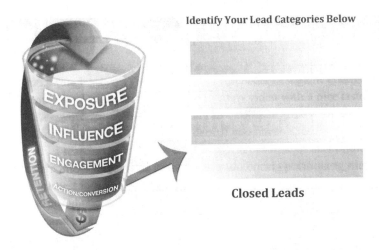

Figure 6.2   *Write the names of your lead categories in the blank spaces.*

List Management

When you're finished with the funnel in Figure 6.2, you should have three or four categories of leads. Next, identify which forms on your website will drive email addresses into each category. This is important for your email list management. Once you have your strategy and content in place, you will want these forms to drop contact information into the correct lists so those leads will receive the correct group of emails. It also will help you reposition existing lists of contacts so they end up in the right email bucket. If you also use a combination of direct mail campaigns, the process is the same. You're trying to identify which lead sources on the website will drive to the new lead categories. As you go through this process, you may find that you need to consolidate some lists or even create new ones to simplify content distribution. A space has been provided to track that as well.

Website Lead Form	Name of Current List	Lead Category	Name of New List

Website Lead Form	Name of Current List	Lead Category	Name of New List

The next step is to identify which communications each list receives today and what you want to change about that based on your new system. In the table that follows, identify the current marketing communications program that leads receive and the primary type of calls to action they get. Then describe how you will modify this as you put your strategy in place.

Name of Current List	Current Primary Call to Action	Name of New List	New Primary Call to Action

Name of Current List	Current Primary Call to Action	Name of New List	New Primary Call to Action

There will still be work to do to ensure that your lead categories are getting the right types of communications at the right times, but if you can correlate your email lists with your lead categories, you can identify quickly whether they're getting the right messages. Then you can integrate any necessary changes into your project plan.

7

Customer Service, Referrals, and Strategies for Increasing Revenue from Existing Customers

Customer retention provides another area in which social media can deliver tremendous value. Customer retention for the purpose of this discussion will focus on activities that are designed to ensure customers are happy, make repeat purchases, and refer new clients. The customer acquisition costs for companies have been on the rise in recent years. Therefore, it's more important than ever to look at how to keep existing customers happy and coming back for more. The mantra is that it's cheaper to keep existing customers than it is to get new ones. Companies are starting to take this seriously, which has led to the increase in adoption of the Net Promoter Score methodology developed by Fred Reichheld, Bain & Company, and Satmetrix. This is a simple method of measuring a customer's likelihood to recommend your product or service on a scale of 1-10. These are categorized into "promoters" who reply with 9-10, "passives" who reply with 7-8, and "detractors" who reply with 0-6. Does a high net promoter score translate into higher revenue? Satmetrix did an analysis of net promoter scores in the computer hardware industry to find out. Based on their research, they showed the total customer worth of a "promoter" was $2,600 based on their repeat purchases and the value of the customers they referred to the company, compared to an average of $1,615. Clearly, promoters have a higher lifetime customer value for companies, showing it's worth working hard to get more of them. How did detractors affect the bottom line? Their customer value was $105, which reflected the decrease in repeat business and the loss of business from others who heard about negative experiences. The research showed that for every six detractors, the company lost five potential customers each year.[1] This study didn't take into account customer acquisition costs, which means that detractors are likely a huge drain on revenue for companies. Social media can be a large contributor to actually generating referrals in this methodology, so Satmetrix recently released a tool to monitor online promoter scores called SparkScore. You can run free reports to see how online sentiment ties to company performance for several industries.

The Net Promoter Score methodology shows there are two clear reasons for keeping your customers happy. First, satisfied customers are more likely to refer business opportunities to your company. Second, happy customers keep coming back for more. From a marketing perspective, customer retention strategies can drive incremental revenue from your customer base by driving incremental purchases from existing customers and increasing customer referrals. The social channel provides an inexpensive, efficient way to manage customer conversations, allowing you to participate in dialogue that helps you better understand your customer base. If you understand your customers, you know what it takes to satisfy them with your products and services. Social media also is a tremendous opportunity to generate loyalty and drive ongoing purchase decisions. This chapter shows you how to manage and empower your customers using social media.

> *There is a place in the world for any business that takes care of its customers—after the sale.*
>
> —Harvey MacKay

Where Customer Retention Fits into the Funnel

As you see in Figure 7.1, customer retention is the big arrow on the back of the funnel, starting at the bottom and wrapping to the top. The sales process doesn't

---

1. http://www.satmetrix.com/pdfs/NP_Economics_Technology_Final.pdf

stop once you have a new customer. The goal is that a new customer will love your product or service so much that he'll come back for more and go through the sales funnel again. Once a new customer is created, there are many ways to market to him. Service and software industries have client on-boarding processes to help new customers know what to expect and have everything they need. Other companies push their customer loyalty programs, such as airline rewards points or coupons for regular customers. These programs are designed to bring back customers more frequently because every time they come back, they spend money.

Figure 7.1   *Where customer retention fits into the sales funnel*

Customer retention is the back side of your sales funnel. Many companies set revenue goals focused on attracting new customers, while ignoring the potential to achieve similar revenue opportunities from customers they already have. And social media can be a big weapon in your arsenal to achieve those revenue goals.

Understanding Customer Retention

Your customers may be talking about you online. Are you listening? They could be saying how amazing your company or product is and getting no response. When customers rave about you, take the time to say thank you. It shows that you're responsive and care about their opinion. However, your customers may also be complaining and pointing out big disconnects in your customer experience. If you aren't keeping track of these conversations, you could be missing information that's crucial to retaining more of your customers. One of marketers' biggest mistakes is thinking that they are their customers. They're so immersed in their companies and in their business, that they think they understand what their customers want. They develop strategies to reach customers based on their own ideas. They forget to actually ask real customers what they want. Social media is an efficient way to do that, and it gives marketers the chance to validate what they think they already know about their customers before investing in a program that could be totally off-base.

Developing a Measureable Strategy for Customer Retention

The following section provides examples of social media strategies that may be effective for increasing customer retention and growing revenue at your organization.

Provide Customer Service

Answering questions and engaging customers' conversations are two of the first things that likely come to mind when you think about customer retention and social media. When customers tweet about a brand, they expect to get a response. And they expect that response to come quickly. Social media has created a real-time dialogue between customers and companies, and it means social media managers have to deal with that dialogue almost immediately. Such real-time customer service can be challenging if teams aren't set up to monitor conversations and respond quickly. Think about who will do your monitoring and responding: If there's a large volume of conversations about your company, it might make the most sense to train your customer service team to manage the dialogue. They are already trained on the policies of the company in managing customers and have all the tools they need except one: training. Many customer service teams don't understand that social media isn't a form-template email; it isn't a place to tell everyone to call your customer service phone number. Complaints have to be managed with care, and it's usually done with a live audience. If you handle the situation well, you might get some cheering. If you handle it poorly, you could get an enraged mob booing and telling all their fans and followers how much you suck.

Training customer service teams on the importance of tone in the twittered word is a critical step. Take a couple of agents who are excellent writers and test them—ask them to respond to a series of test complaints in 140 characters or less, as the space limits of Twitter make conveying the right tone a challenge. If they pass muster, they earn the right to monitor the social conversation. If they don't, you test more people until you feel that you'll be able to sleep at night without worrying that a clueless customer service agent is going to create a firestorm on one of your social networks.

One rogue customer service agent mishandling social media can destroy relationships with multiple paying customers, and replacing lost customers is expensive, especially for small companies.

You would expect a company selling customer relationship management (CRM) software to understand that. Unfortunately, that wasn't the case with CRM software provider Solve360.

I tried to call Solve360 to ask a highly technical question about its software integration with an email provider. I had scoured the company's website for an answer and didn't find it in the help section. So I found a customer service phone number, called, and pressed 2 for customer service. I got a voice mailbox. I thought maybe that if I pressed 1 for sales, the company would be more likely to answer the phone. (Many times, I've found that companies' sales lines get better attention.) So I called back and pressed 1 for sales. I got voicemail again, and it actually asked me to "most importantly" leave my email address so Solve360 could answer my question. Why have a customer service telephone number if it's just going to a voicemail that asks for your customer's email address? I had a technical question, and I really needed human conversation, so I sent the tweet shown in Figure 7.2.

Nichole_Kelly
Mar 21, 2:46pm via Tweet Button
Experience w @solve360 Call, get voice system. Press 1 for sales, get voicemail! Leave a message w ur email & we'll be in touch. #fail

Figure 7.2 *Solve360's voice message says the most important thing to leave is your email address.*

I had a good feeling that I would receive an email response even though I only left the nature of the question on the voicemail and asked Solve360 to call me to discuss it. I left my email address and phone number. The company sent an email that didn't remotely address my question because it didn't know what the question was. Then Solve360 sent me a link to its help center. I was extremely frustrated but ready to give up and let it go. I tweeted as much and received the response, as shown in Figure 7.3, from Solve360.

solve360
Mar 21, 6:48pm via Web
@Nichole_Kelly Squeaky wheels don't get greased here.
Hide conversation

Figure 7.3 *Solve360's response to a complaint was offensive and a great example of what not to do.*

My jaw hit the floor. I retweeted it, noting that it was how *not* to handle customer service. This set off a firestorm of tweets from people who were appalled at Solve360. You would think it ended there, but the company decided the best course of action was to start attacking people who were involved in the conversation, as shown in Figure 7.4.

Figure 7.4   *Solve360 attacks followers who commented.*

The story continued, and tweets and emails were exchanged. Megan Horn posted her entire experience on her blog, including the email she received from Solve360's founder that blamed her for jumping into a conversation that she wasn't a part of and insulted her by stating that social media would never be a top-10 business driver.

The reason to review this experience isn't to bash Solve360 but to illustrate how dangerous it can be when the wrong person is managing your corporate social media channels. In Solve360's case, it would have been better not to respond at all than to go on a tirade that ultimately resulted in the company abandoning its Twitter account for several weeks because it claimed "the cool kids ruined it." Instead, Solve360 focused on LinkedIn, where "real people do business." Solve360 probably did get more buzz than it ever had before, but none of it was positive, and people started to question whether the company understood the industry it served. So, when choosing someone to manage your social media customer service, choose wisely. There are other factors to consider when putting together your customer service strategy. First, decide when it's appropriate to take the conversation to another medium of communication. It's tough to handle an entire inquiry within the 140-character limits of Twitter. But that doesn't mean you should answer every tweet with a customer service phone number or a request for an email. The customer has reached out to you; don't put the responsibility for following up about an issue back on the customer.

The small business CRM provider Infusionsoft understands the importance of providing clear answers quickly in social channels. Infusionsoft's responses cut to the chase and directly address the questions at hand. When a customer needs more help, the company respond with resources directly relevant to the customer's question, as shown in Figure 7.5.

Figure 7.5   *Infusionsoft answers questions directly and sends to web resources for more complicated answers.*

Joseph Manna, Infusionsoft's community manager, said, "We use social media as a contact channel where we are very candid. Customers don't have a problem sharing exactly how they feel at 10 p.m. at night on Twitter. It gives us an opportunity to reach out to them, contact them, and make sure they end up happy." Through its personalized help and support, Infusionsoft has not only been able to retain customers, but turned customers into advocates for Infusionsoft. The company prides itself not only on giving the most accurate answer, but on answering as quickly as possible. Manna went on to say: "I had an experience with Rackspace where I had a response of 11 seconds. I was extremely impressed, and we are striving for a similar response time at Infusionsoft."

Infusionsoft also understands that it will answer the same types of questions many times. Therefore, it leverages a robust knowledge base on its website. The knowledge base provides a searchable resource and a self-service help center for customers. So, its customer service team is a click, a call, an email, a tweet, or a status update away. The team understands the need to provide complete responses— quickly. And when a status update or a tweet isn't enough room, the team will either link you to an existing article in that extensive knowledge base, or—when necesssary—write a new article addressing your question and link you to that.

For Infusionsoft, this streamlines the response process because the team doesn't have to write the same answers over and over. For its customers, it has built a valuable resource that uncovers answers to questions quickly and efficiently. The knowledge base has a robust search tool that searches its help articles, its community forums, its user guide, its video library, and its blog for the answer. It also helps that the link to that knowledge base is available right within Infusionsoft's software.

To take it a step further, Infusionsoft also extensively uses YouTube to provide training and tutorial videos, as shown in Figure 7.6. Joseph stated, "video is an important part of our customer service. We sell software, and we've found that customers appreciate being able to see the answer to their question being demonstrated." Infusionsoft also highlights customer stories in video case studies that provide the opportunity to expose its small business clients and demonstrate real-life examples of how its tools are being used. Though Infusionsoft isn't formerly measuring its net promoter score currently, it is certainly taking actions to ensure its bottom line sees the benefits of happy customers.

Figure 7.6 *Infusionsoft uses YouTube to tell customer stories like this video of customer Pam Slim.*

If customers are talking about you on social media channels, you should build a strategy on how to participate in the conversation. There are two sides of this equation. The first is customer service. The other, equally important, side is product and service innovation. Social media conversations can gauge what your customers really want from your product. What features would they add? What would they change? Where is your product line lacking? Your customers may have the answers to these questions, and many times they'll be happy to tell you.

Part of this is reactionary. You will recognize opportunities to fix processes, change product offerings, and even add service offerings based on customers' questions. You can prioritize your actions based on the level of conversation about particular issues. This can be extremely important because when you act in response to customers' feedback, you have an opportunity to tell the customers who inspired the change. Customers love to hear that they were listened to; it will go a long way in deepening your bond. Social media also provides you a platform to ask questions of customers you wouldn't ordinarily hear from. They may hate something about your product or service, but they aren't likely to tell you—unless you ask. You may be amazed at the types of suggestions you get.

Turn Customers into Revenue

Providing better customer service through the social channel is great, but you'll still run into the same question from your management team: How is this delivering on the bottom line? It's simple, really, and it's why companies already market to their existing customers. Happy customers generate revenue.

There are three ways you can increase revenue from existing customers:

- You can increase the number of referrals for new business from your existing customers.
- You can increase the amount existing customers spend at each purchase.
- You can work to get existing customers to purchase more frequently.

We'll use the example of a business-to-business (B2B) software company to illustrate this. You could put together a referral incentive program for customers to drive software purchases from your customer's network of qualified buyers. This would drive more referrals and ultimately more sales if implemented properly. Or, if the software company were to put together a promotional program to drive sales of add-on products for its software, it would increase the amount that existing customers are spending. Finally, the same company could offer a program that provides a discount or special extras if customers renew their license within 30 days after a product upgrade is released. This drives current customers to purchase more frequently. One of the big challenges in the software industry is adoption of new upgrades, so the more customers they can get upgraded immediately after a release, the better the revenue pipeline becomes. This is one of the driving forces behind the software as a service model. Software as a service revolves around providing the software for a monthly or annual fee. Users don't have to upgrade because new product releases are automatically rolled out to users. But for the software company, it provides predictable and recurring cash flow.

This is also true for service industries. An advertising agency could offer credits toward a client's fees for referring new business, or it could offer to add services at a discounted rate for each client referral. Many times companies bring on an advertising agency for a specific set of services, but the agency may offer a whole suite of services that the client isn't using. Companies could put together a program ensuring that clients understand the other types of services they offer to encourage add-on sales. This encourages clients to spend more each month.

Finally, agencies could create a new revenue stream through training offerings for their clients that would encourage incremental monthly revenue for products that aren't direct client services but would increase the frequency of purchases.

Use Referral Strategies

Social media has transformed word-of-mouth marketing. Where it used to be that Jane would call you up and ask who your favorite airline is, today you can see Jane's comments about her favorite airline on any of her social networks. Rather than telling your 10 closest friends what you think about a company, now you can tell hundreds or thousands (some can tell millions) with a few simple keystrokes. This can work for or against your company. Negative comments travel faster than ever before. But social media has leveled the playing field for positive feedback. Historically, horror stories spread like wildfire, whereas positive feedback went unnoticed. What we see today is that when friends share a positive experience, their friends jump in to add their own perspective. This dialogue helps the story spread, and even a slew of passive bystanders will "like" someone's story about a positive experience. It's so easy to throw a little kudos to a company that it's happening more and more often.

Every positive comment is an opportunity for referral business. The big question is whether a company can track the new business back to the individual who referred it. Social referrals can be big business—so much so that software companies like Social Share App are developing entire software platforms around it.

Virgin Mobile understands the power of a referral. For cell phone companies, referrals mean a lot of money. That's likely why Virgin Mobile promoted its referral program right on a Facebook tab and even offered substantial prizes to encourage customers to participate, as shown in Figure 7.7. Facilitating online referrals is no different from facilitating an online lead—you need to make it stupidly easy for people, on the company blog, on the Facebook page, from Twitter. But referral "programs" aren't the secret sauce of acquiring customers in social media channels.

Think about the last time you recommended a brand. Did you do it because a promotion encouraged you to? Or did you do it because you just want your friends to know whom you trust? It's likely the latter. When you see good customer service or have an amazing experience, you're inclined to talk about it. And it's not usually because you have a super affinity to any brand, although in some cases that develops over time. You do it because you care about your friends. If one of your friends has a problem, you want to help him find a solution—and your company might be that solution. This is an explicit referral, and it certainly is one part of the equation. But more often, there are implicit referrals—the referrals that happen because you share a piece of content that you like, and one of your followers sees it and needs what you offer. This is likely happening every day for your company, and you may not have even begun to consider how to quantify the impact. How do you track when a new prospect reaches out to your company because she saw you provide excellent customer service on social media? Infusionsoft has seen this in action, "a by-product of taking care of our customers is that just the conversation alone will generate interest from their friends that are like them. They see our conversations and reach out to find out more about what we do. That is the starting point of a new relationship."

Figure 7.7 *Virgin Mobile uses a Facebook tab to drive referrals.*

But how could you track the business that comes from social referrals back to the referrer? What does it require? The answer is much simpler than it sounds—a unique URL that is tied to the individual who shared it. But how do you accomplish that?

The social sharing platform SocialToaster has mastered this art. It offers a unique platform that allows people to sign up to become brand ambassadors, or what they call "super fans." When you share content through SocialToaster's tool, your super fans receive an email that shows what content you've shared with them. At the bottom of the email is a big Click to Share button. If the super fan clicks the button, it automatically shares the content on his social networks. This is SocialToaster's big differentiator. It is seeing that about 70% of its clients actually share the content *on their own social networks*. SocialToaster'system then tracks which traffic each person sent to your website and which traffic resulted in conversions. Even better, it provides a list of your top ambassadors. This is extremely powerful data when developing outreach strategies.

A Baltimore-based furniture store, Shofer's, recognized the potential and launched a VIP Customer program using the tool (see Figure 7.8). Its goal was to implement a dynamic website and social marketing campaign to drive sales to the store, promote product offerings, and complement the retailer's pre-existing television and print campaign. In six months, the program was responsible for a 400% increase in website traffic. Shofer's found that each ambassador who shared content drove an average of seven new website visitors. As a result of this increase in site traffic, Shofer's has experienced a significant increase in both web leads and overall store sales, both of which are tracked by SocialToaster's reporting feature.

Figure 7.8   *Shofer's Furniture uses brand ambassadors to drive implicit referrals.*

When you think about building a referral strategy, consider how you should drive both implicit and explicit referrals.

Spend More Money at Each Purchase

Another option is to develop a program that encourages customers to spend more every time they make a purchase. The gift retailer Thirty-One Gifts provides Facebook fans with an incentive designed to do this, as shown in Figure 7.9. It offers a steeply discounted tote bag for every $31 spent. This encourages customers to spend more to get their first and even second tote for $5. Customers who have selected purchases that total close to $30 or $60 have a great incentive to cross the threshold so they can get their extra tote. With social media, this should extend beyond a simple offer for a larger ticket sale. You can also combine social media promotions with email marketing campaigns that drive purchases.

Figure 7.9 *Retailer Thirty-One Gifts gives discounts on add-on products based on the amount its customers spend.*

Make More Frequent Purchases

Finally, the last option is to focus on getting customers to buy more often. If average customers purchase your product once a year, you would develop a strategy that encouraged them to make two purchases a year. This is the premise behind the cards many restaurants hand out that reward you with something free after you get a certain number of punches on your VIP or loyalty card.

The shoe retailer JustFab uses a subscription model for shoe purchases to drive monthly sales, as shown in Figure 7.10. VIP members receive an email with recommendations for their monthly purchase selected by their personal shopper. Members can select which shoe they want for their $39.95 monthly fee or choose to skip the month. Every month, JustFab announces the latest styles on its Facebook page with stunning pictures. It also has a community-driven photo gallery where clients take pictures of themselves trying on their shoes for the first time, which increases exposure as clients' friends see their unique styles. The combination of using a subscription model, involving customers on the company's Facebook page and in the community, and integrating personalized email selections led to $25 million in sales in 2011, and the company is reported to be on track for $100 million in sales in 2012.[2]

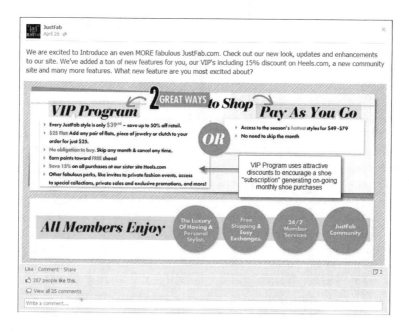

Figure 7.10 *Online shoe retailer JustFab uses a monthly shoe subscription to increase purchase frequency.*

---

2. BetaKit (http://betakit.com/2012/04/26/on-track-for-100m-in-sales-justfab-adds-features-and-launches-in-germany)

Define Your Goal for Customer Retention

Did any of these strategies make a light bulb appear for you? Do you see opportunities to use social media to keep your customers happy? Is there a potential to drive incremental revenues from existing customers? Before you dive in, take the time to research where your customers are—don't scramble to launch a Facebook strategy if your customers aren't even there. Instead, as a first step, stop and ask your customers which social networks they participate on. A quick email survey of your customer base could be incredibly insightful.

Listen

All strategies should start with listening. Remember, you aren't your customer. Listening to the conversation on social channels may give you an idea of what your customers are looking for, or it may show that your customers never talk about you. Either way, listening will help drive your strategy in a direction that will be a win-win for you and your customers.

If you find a large volume of complaints about your company, take them seriously—each complaint is an opportunity to fix a problem. Look for trends and themes in these complaints and see what you need to change to prevent the problem from happening again. Do not take a defensive tone in response to these complaints. Instead, use Chris Brogan's approach to acknowledge, apologize, and act so it's clear you want to solve the problem.

Define Success Metrics

When you have a general idea of which direction you want to take, define the metrics you will use to measure success. Customer retention strategies have a variety of metrics to show progress through the sales funnel. As you review these metrics, think about the life cycle of the customer and how someone progresses through the funnel. With customer retention, there are new metrics to consider.

Referrals	Service	Revenue/Sales	Retention
These metrics are calculated for customers who interacted with the social channel at some point in their customer life cycle.			
Impressions	Time to resolution	Total sales volume	Retention rate
Engagement	# of customers serviced in social	Total revenue	Average time retained as active customer
Soft lead	# of customer saves on social	Average revenue per customer	Lifetime value of customer

Referrals	Service	Revenue/Sales	Retention
These metrics are calculated for customers who interacted with the social channel at some point in their customer life cycle.			
Hard lead	Cost to service	Average sales per customer	Frequency of engagement in social channel
Purchases	Percent use of online self-help versus offline customer support	Average revenue per transaction	
		Average sales units per transaction	
		Frequency of purchase	
		Conversion rate	

* Referral metrics are simplified into the lead generation categories discussed previously. Review lead generation metrics for the full list.

A few metrics in this list require further explanation. These metrics are most commonly used to measure the success of customer service teams and are important to consider for social media customer service strategies. You can compare them across online and offline customer service options to show how social media affects core service metrics.

Customer Saves

Customer saves are defined as the number of customers who were considering switching or were identified as potential defectors to a competitor who were saved because of social media involvement.

Cost to Service

The *cost to service* is defined as the expenses required to serve a customer online versus the cost that would have been incurred for offline customer service options.

Percent Use of Online Self-Help Versus Offline Customer Support

Customers who interact in the social channel will likely still use offline customer service options. This metric calculates the percentage of support that is provided online versus offline. This helps to demonstrate whether social media is driving customers to use online self-help options more often than customers who do not interact with the social channel.

Define Your Strategy

The next step is to create a few options for your strategy. It's your opportunity to use your creative genius about how your company could improve customer retention and customer revenue channels through the social channel. Think about which social channels your customers participate in and ask, "Is it appropriate for my company to engage them there?" Although you may have several customers on Facebook, it may not be the appropriate place to engage them in conversation about your product or service. It may not be a place where you can add value. For example, even though you're an active user on Facebook, you may have no interest in engaging in dialogue with your sewage company there. Most of us don't want to know where sewage goes and certainly aren't searching for our sewage company's fan page. If your sewage company wanted to engage in conversation on Facebook, it would probably be a better approach to go through a news outlet, where their customers are more likely to be open to their announcements.

As you monitor the social landscape, remember that the social networks getting a lot of press (like Twitter and Facebook) may not be where your customers are. "The Conversation Report: What Consumers Are Saying About Banking" released by Social Media Explorer revealed that more than 90% of conversations related to consumers' views on the banking industry were within forums and message boards. For the banking industry, a Twitter strategy is less important than a presence on forums and message boards where customers actually participate. Don't forget to consider your approach for your corporate blog and private online community, if you have one. Broaden your focus to consider other types of social networks that may not be as cool or cutting edge but that represent a large chunk of conversations about your company or industry.

After you've evaluated which social networks are important, think about how you can use them to add value. Is there a need for ongoing customer service? Would your customers benefit from useful resources like Infusionsoft provides? Where do you think you can save your company money by engaging customers in the social channel? How could you engage your audience to drive incremental revenue? Come up with a few ideas that you can take to the next stage in the planning process.

Example Strategy A:

Improve customer retention and complaint resolution online

Example Strategy B:

Increase customer referrals from the social channel

Example Strategy C:

Drive customers engaged in the social channel to make more frequent purchases

Remember, the first step of the strategy process is to define what you're trying to accomplish. You may jump to creating a tactic like, "we'll provide service online" without identifying why that makes sense for your organization and what you're trying to achieve by providing service online. The best strategies are designed to generate a specific business impact that is clearly defined. That's what makes them measureable strategies. This part of the process identifies *why* you're going down this path. Your creative process will naturally try to leapfrog this stage and jump to the how. This is one of the primary reasons that executives have a hard time understanding where social media fits into the organization. Their brains are wired to understand why something needs to be done, first and foremost. They will prioritize initiatives based on whether your argument for why is compelling. By defining the why first, you're more likely to identify something that's truly important to the business. When you jump to defining what you want to do and try to back in the why, executives tend to tune out.

Define How You Will Do It

Be creative about how to achieve the strategy you select. The simple answer to the first strategy is to add, "We will improve customer retention and complaint resolution online by deploying customer service protocols when our brand is mentioned on forums and message boards." You should probably do that, but do other options get your creative juices flowing? How will you differentiate yourselves from your competitors? Create ideas that align with the mind-set of your customers, fulfill their needs, and make them say, "Wow!" Brainstorm, and put everything down on paper—there are no wrong answers here. If you discount an idea before it can even form completely, you'll miss a great opportunity.

Flesh It Out

When you have a pretty full sheet of paper (or white board), evaluate your ideas for feasibility, budget needs, and anticipated impact. Which will have the greatest effect with the least amount of resource requirements? What can you do immediately? Which ideas require a ramp-up period? Think about the first five things that need to happen to make the idea a reality and create a mini action plan. Drop ideas that aren't fitting the bill and focus on the two or three that have the most promise.

Organize Your Plans

Now that you have your top two or three strategies, start building your action plans. Define the resources you need, the departments that need to be involved, and the tasks that need to be accomplished. Look at the timing of implementation and align it with your company's other initiatives so you have a realistic implementation schedule.

Create Planning Documents

The process is the same no matter which type of strategy you're developing. The next step is to create your high-level road map and project plans for your strategy.

12-Month High-Level Road Map

This document prioritizes your initiatives and their associated tactics over a 12-month period, as seen in Figure 7.11. It helps to set expectations around the level of work required and identifies the necessary resources. This document is great to share with management teams and outside vendors because it provides a single-page glance at your plan over a year. If needed, it also can identify budgets for each of the initiatives broken down by expense category.

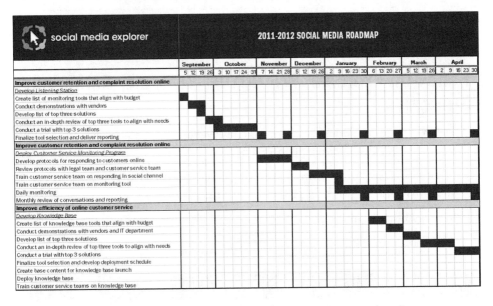

Figure 7.11 *Develop a high-level road map for your strategies and tactics.*

Tactical Project Plan

The tactical plan is simply a project plan, as shown in Figure 7.12. It lays out all the tasks that need to be accomplished, the anticipated completion dates, and who is responsible for completing them. It's typically completed for an upcoming quarter and adjusted based on the progress each month.

Project Plan	Target Date	Responsible	Completion Date
January SME Tasks			
Select Social Media Monitoring Software			
Conduct a needs analysis with client			
Define client needs			
Send client needs analysis report for review			
Adjust needs analysis report based on client feedback			
Finalize needs analysis document and send for approval			
Create list of SMMS vendors for review			
Conduct demonstrations with vendors to align features with client needs			
Develop SMMS vendor features and client needs analysis matrix			
Write up recommendations for top 3 SMMS vendors			
Conduct in-depth demonstrations with top 3 SMMS vendors			
Set up 30 day trial period with top 3 SMMS vendors			
Deploy team to review top 3 SMMS vendors during trial period with SME and client			
Meeting to discuss trial period client feedback			
Write up recommendation for the SMMS vendor that aligns best with client needs			
Include Pros and Cons for vendor selection			
Include Budgetary Requirements and Vendor Contract			
January Client Tasks			
Select Social Media Monitoring Software			
Review needs analysis report and send feedback to SME			
Approve needs analysis document			
Conduct in-depth demonstrations with top 3 SMMS vendors with SME			
Select employees for trial period with SMMS vendors			
Provide SME with feedback on top 3 vendors			
Finalize contract with selected SMMS vendor			

Figure 7.12   *The tactical plan lays out tasks on a granular level to identify the project scope.*

Hands-On Exercise: Prioritizing Customer Retention Strategies

Just as you did with brand awareness and lead generation strategies, you need to prioritize your customer retention strategies.

These worksheets are designed to help you go through the brainstorming process and provide a framework for prioritizing your ideas.

Strategy Evaluation Matrix

In the box, document your proposed strategy.

Proposed Strategy

In the following table, list the reasons you think the idea is awesome. Then write down all the things that could go wrong, hold back success, or utterly kibosh the impact. (These may be internal or external factors.) Finally, rate the potential impact of your idea on the company on a scale of 1 to 5. 1 means very little impact, and 5 means a tremendous impact. When you consider impact, remember you need to relate the impact to core business goals, increased sales volume, increased revenue, or decreased costs. Ultimately, you can determine the criteria to measure the potential impact, but remember that you have to use the same criteria across all the strategies you're considering.

Pros	Cons	Potential Impact

Once you've gone through this exercise with each strategy idea, evaluate another set of criteria: feasibility. You might have a fantastic idea for a large online customer service team, but if you work for a small start-up, the idea isn't feasible. In the table that follows, rate the level of resources required to execute the strategy. Move on to risk, and consider the risks your strategy could create for the company—is there very little risk, or could a mistake lead to a lawsuit? Could this strategy have a huge effect on customer referrals with little to no risk?

Rate from 1 to 5. 1 = Least, 5 = Most			
Top Three Strategies	Level of Effort	Risk	Impact

You can't make decisions based solely on your company's aversion to risk; however, it's important to understand your own confidence levels and what types of risk you need to mitigate. If you develop a plan to increase feasibility, mitigate risk, and have a strong confidence level, you'll be prepared for your management team's questions. Other types of strategies may have a low level of effort but a substantially positive impact. You may want to move those to the top of the list when you consider the same criteria for other strategies.

8

Measuring Strategies for Increasing Revenue from Existing Customers

Although there is a clear-cut set of metrics associated with customer retention, measuring the impact of social media programs on retention can be challenging. The best measurements require you to identify which customers interacted on social media within your customer relationship management (CRM) system. Although this may be a barrier to getting some of the most insightful metrics, it doesn't preclude you from showing progress and value in some core metrics that matter to the organization. Even if you can never identify customers who touched the social channel in your CRM, you can use a more general approach to draw conclusions about the role social media is playing in your success. This chapter will help you identify the metrics you can get today and the data you need to figure out a way to collect.

Where Customer Revenue Generation Strategies Fit into the Organization

A social media customer retention strategy typically requires collaboration between the social media team and the customer service department. This may be the first time that a marketing strategy requires such an intensive partnership between its social media marketers and customer service agents. This is exciting for teams that enjoy collaboration, but it can present a challenge for teams that usually work in isolation. Territorial battles may hinder your ability to get buy-in for your ideas. This will make it even more important to have a clear objective measured in terms of financial return. If you can present your idea as a way to help the customer service department meet its goals, you become an ally and not an adversary, and it's much easier to get cooperation. To do this, you need to understand the objectives your customer service team is held accountable to.

> *Always think of your customers as suppliers first. Work closely with them, so they can supply you with the information you need to supply them with the right products and services.*
>
> —Susan Marthaller

Finding Your Key Metrics

If your goal is to show how social media can affect customer service and customer retention metrics, the first place you should look is at the customer service report. From that report, make a list of the metrics that measure their success—call volume, call time, calls handled, cost per call, resolution rate, and hold times in organizations with a customer service call center. In other organizations, you may find metrics that are more operations—focused—time to resolution, response rate, time to response, and the number of interactions with a customer before a resolution was delivered. You will find some golden nuggets in these reports that you can equally measure and provide improvements through the social channel.

Another area to find important metrics is in your executive-level customer report. These reports have metrics like average revenue per customer, average sales volume per customer, average profit per customer, total customer revenue, total customer sales volume, and net profit. Many times this report focuses on detailed metrics that roll into a standard profit and loss statement—also known as an income statement or P&L. If you aren't familiar with these reports, Google "income statement" or "profit and loss statement" to find some samples.

You may have to approach senior management to get these reports, and they can be close-mouthed with figures. One approach that may be successful is, "I'm trying to get a handle on the metrics that are important to the customer service team to see if there's an opportunity for us to help them reach their goals."

Manager Metrics

There's a difference between the metrics that are important to managers and the metrics that are important to executives. This distinction is one of the most important takeaways from this book. For customer retention, manager-level metrics focus on engagement with customers in the social channel. There's a transition between the time the engagement occurs with the customer and what happens downstream in the customer life cycle that can be correlated with your engagement.

Monthly Manager Metrics			
Overall Customer Engagement on Social Channels	**Customer Service on Social Channels**	**Referrals from Social Channels**	**Customer Sales Promotions on Social Channels**
# of brand mentions from customers	# of mentions with positive or neutral sentiment	# of brand mentions from customers	# of views of sales promotion
# of clicks on customer-specific content	# of mentions with negative sentiment	# of new conversations from customer mention	# of shares of sales promotion
# of shares of customer-specific content	# of complaints handled	# of soft leads generated from customer mentions	# of soft conversions from sales promotion
# of site visits referred from customer-specific content	# of complaints with positive outcome	# of hard leads generated from customer mentions	# of hard conversions from sales promotion
# of site calls to action completed from customer-specific content	Average time to response	Total incremental sales volume generated from customer mentions	Total incremental sales volume generated
		Total incremental revenue generated from customer mentions	Total incremental revenue generated
		Conversion rate	Conversion rate

Note: If you're unfamiliar with the difference between a soft and a hard conversion, review the chapters on lead generation.

The next set of metrics focuses on reviewing the effect the social channel is having on the lifetime value of a customer. The first thing you'll notice is that there's a category to measure retention for leads that originated in the social channel. Although this wasn't discussed at depth in this chapter, it was reviewed in the lead generation chapters. Typically, the reporting for lead generation strategies will bleed into your retention reports to show the lifetime value of the customers that were generated.

Year-to-Date Manager-Level Lead Source Metrics	Client Acquired from Social Referral	Client Interacted with Social Media Prior to Purchase Only	Client Interacted with Social Media After Purchase Only	Client Interacted with Social Media Before and After Purchase	Client Never Interacted with the Social Channel
These metrics are calculated for customers who interacted with the social channel at some point in their customer life cycle.					
Total YTD sales volume					
Total YTD revenue					
Average sales volume per customer					
Average revenue per customer					
Retention rate					
Average months retained as active customer					
Lifetime value of customer					
Average customer service costs per customer					

These metrics provide a holistic view of the day-to-day metrics that matter and the metrics that show the long-term value of your efforts. You should compare these metrics against the same set of metrics for customers who have never interacted with the social channel so you can see if there are areas where social is making a substantial difference.

Executive Metrics

The way to your executive team's heart is through dollars and cents. Therefore, you roll certain manager-level metrics into business objective metrics that show where your social strategy is providing the most value to the organization. The last column is dedicated to responses from your existing customers to promotions that were sent through social channels. This is typically created by comparing the customer list of those who responded to a promotion to the prior customer list to see how many existing customers responded.

Monthly Executive Metrics			
Overall Customer Engagement on Social Channels	Customer Service on Social Channels	Referrals from Social Channels	Customer Sales Promotions on Social Channels
Cost per customer engagement	% of positive versus negative sentiment	Cost per soft lead generated from customer mentions	Cost per soft conversion from sales promotion
	Cost per customer served	Cost per hard lead generated from customer mentions	Cost per hard conversion from sales promotion
	Cost per complaint handled	Total incremental sales volume generated from customer mentions	Total incremental sales volume generated
	# of complaints with positive outcome	Total incremental revenue generated from customer mentions	Total incremental revenue generated
	Average time to response	Conversion rate	Conversion rate

Executives want to understand how social media is affecting the company's ability to retain customers who interact with the social channel. Therefore, you will use a simplified version of the lead source report to highlight the key metrics they care about.

Year-to-Date Executive-Level Lead Source Metrics					
	Client Acquired from Social Referral	Client Interacted with Social Media Prior to Purchase Only	Client Interacted with Social Media After Purchase Only	Client Interacted with Social Media Before and After Purchase	Client Never Interacted with the Social Channel
These metrics are calculated for customers who interacted with the social channel at some point in their customer life cycle.					
Total YTD sales volume					
Total YTD revenue					
Average sales volume per customer					
Average revenue per customer					
Retention rate					
Lifetime value of customer					
Average customer service costs per customer					

You also can use your manager-level reports to pull out key insights and share them as highlights in the overview for your executive report. When you compare how social media affected these core metrics against the same metrics for customers who had no participation in the social media channel, you may find important information. For example, you may find a substantial increase in the retention rate or average revenue generated per customer when they engage in the social channel. Make sure you highlight these in a summary of key findings and attach it to your report.

Why This Is Going to Be Difficult but Not Impossible

Unfortunately, you can't snap your fingers and produce all this data. However, some pieces are easier than others. Getting most of the manager-level data to show the number of interactions and sentiment from your customers is a little easier. But reporting on sales volume and revenue will start to identify road blocks. Getting this level of insight may require changes in some of your business process and data storage methods. It requires that you be able to separate customers who have interacted with the social channel from those who haven't in your CRM system. You may not be able to do that today, but it is neither impossible nor as hard as everyone makes it out to be. But you need to be able to quickly identify the barriers and understand which dots you're trying to connect. When you're empowered with an understanding of basic systems and how they connect, sometimes simple solutions surface. In the next chapter, you'll learn how to identify the barriers to successfully getting to the data you need and how to overcome them.

What If You Can't Separate Customers Who Touch Your Social Media Channels?

In an ideal world, you would know exactly which of your customers interacted in the social channel. In reality, that may not be possible in the short term. The big question is, "Should I not pursue a customer retention strategy if I can't connect data from the social channel to my CRM system?" Of course you should; you can use plenty of other metrics to look for trends that correlate to your social media involvement. If you can't isolate the social channel, look for improvements in those metrics across all customers before and after you deployed your strategy. Although you can't definitively say that social media was the reason for the improvement, you can certainly show the before and after. Be prepared for some skepticism from your executive team: "Are we sure it wasn't hiring Suzy that decreased our average response time?" or "Aren't people who use social media sites more likely to find their answer online with or without social media's involvement?" You need to be prepared with case studies from other companies and industry-level stats to attempt to defray these types of comments. If you can't find case studies or statistics to support your position, you may have to bring in an objective third party who understands social media and your business to add credibility to your findings. It's ridiculous that an outsider can come in and say the same thing you've been saying forever and turn on light bulbs with your management team, but sometimes it's the reality of office politics.

Hands-On Exercise: Finding Customer Retention Metrics

The first step in aligning social media with customer retention is to understand how success is measured today. Remember, you aren't going to create a dashboard of fancy social media metrics that no one else understands. Instead, you'll find core metrics that have history and baselines for success established in the company.

Getting the Reports You Need

Pull together some existing reports in your organization. You'll use these reports to define metrics that you think will have a positive effect on your strategy. Do a little recon work to get insight into how other departments are measured.

Find a way to gather the following reports:

- Customer Service Department Daily/Weekly/Monthly Reporting
- Customer Service Department Executive Report
- Customer Loyalty Program Manager Report
- Customer Loyalty Program Executive Report
- Referral Program Manager Report
- Referral Program Executive Report
- Daily and Monthly Company Level Executive Summary Report
- Operations Department Daily/Weekly/Monthly Reporting
- Operations Department Executive Report

Some companies separate the operations and customer service department, so reports from both departments are listed. The operations department is usually focused on cutting costs and increasing productivity in the organization. Social media may be able to help do both, so you want to understand the areas the operations department is focused on. Your company may call these reports a variety of different names but focus on the reports that show the type of data you've seen throughout the chapter.

After you have the reports, pull out the key metrics that you can affect the most. You may chose to measure all of them in the beginning to figure out where the greatest impact is, but you want to start with a hypothesis of where you're trying to move the needle.

Key Metrics That Social Media Can Affect				
Customer Service Report	Operations Report	Customer Loyalty Program Report	Referral Program Report	Executive Report

Key Metrics That Social Media Can Affect				
Customer Service Report	Operations Report	Customer Loyalty Program Report	Referral Program Report	Executive Report

After you know which metrics you want to collect, you need to understand where the metric is stored so you can find a way to integrate social data. In the following exercise, list the metrics you identified as possibilities and track the report the metrics came from. Then ask where the data was pulled from and where the original data is stored. In companies that use a data warehouse or have sophisticated reporting systems, you may find that these are very different systems. Finally, ask if there's a way to cross-reference social media data with these existing reports. Be prepared that the answer may be no for now. In Chapters 9 and 10, you'll receive several tips to overcome the barriers and get the data you need.

Key Metrics Systems Analysis				
Metric	Found in This Report	System Where Data Was Pulled	System Where Data Is Stored	Social Media Data Integration?

In the next exercise, you'll correlate the new information you've received with what is possible today and what you need to work toward. In the first column, identify the metrics that are available today. In the second column, designate whether you can isolate customers who touch the social media channel when you pull that metric. Next, list the metrics that you could get to with a little effort. This may require the purchase of a new tool, a software add-on for your CRM system, or a small custom development project. In the final column, list the metrics that are almost impossible to get to because either the systems don't talk to each other or the level of effort required to get to the data is far too great to justify the effort. These are called the metrics that require you to move heaven and earth. You want to keep these metrics on your radar because as systems improve, you may find that suddenly they become much easier to report on.

Metrics Available Today	Social Media Isolation Possible? Yes or No	Metrics Available with Small Effort	Metrics That Require You to Move Heaven and Earth

II

Tools for Collecting Metrics

9

Breaking Down the Barriers to Social Media Measurement

If measuring social media were easy, everyone would be doing it. Instead, marketers are struggling to measure return on investment (ROI) without any real indication of where the problems lie. Let's face it—marketers went for decades without being held accountable to core metrics. Executives viewed marketing as a necessary evil, so they let marketers get away with presenting fluff. Then came the recession that started in 2008. Businesses started bleeding capital and losing sales, so executives started asking marketers tough questions: Which programs were actually delivering a return? This put marketers on notice. They needed to show some results or prepare to see their budgets shrink drastically. By early 2009, articles focused on "recessionary" marketing started popping up, with topics like "How to Get the Most Out of Your Marketing Budget in a Recession." Although the recession is fading, the pragmatic mind-set has not. The push to market smarter and increase the success of existing marketing programs took center stage away from the "shiny and expensive new idea" mind-set that held sway for so long.

This pushed social media to the forefront, and for the next few years, marketers considered it the go-to cost-effective marketing solution. Indeed, they even considered it a "free" marketing program. But marketers quickly realized that social media programs were enormous drains on their staffs' time. The costs started to surface as marketers hired new employees to manage their social media presence or outsourced some of the most time-intensive social media tasks—like content development. Since then, measuring ROI has become the top question for marketers.[1] So why haven't we figured it out?

The truth is, marketing communications folks aren't really measurement junkies. Memorable marketing campaigns are based on outstanding creative ideas that break through the cluttered media market. Therefore, many successful marketers are creative types who thrive on the brainstorming session and the generation of ideas. They're the types who would rather claw their eyes out than sit in front of a spreadsheet for hours trying to manipulate data. But the reality is that success in marketing now requires just that, and marketers are faced with a seemingly endless learning curve. The natural next step is to look for a tool to perform the measurement, to generate reports that appear miraculously in the inbox and contain the answers to every burning question the executives have. Here's why that hasn't happened yet.

> *Most marketing communications folks would rather claw their eyes out than sit in front of a spreadsheet for hours trying to manipulate data.*

You Are the Problem

Sometimes it's tough to look yourself in the mirror and admit that you've caused a problem that you can't find a solution for, but the majority of people who say social media can't be measured use arguments that are full of holes. The most common argument has been that the metric ROI doesn't show where social media is delivering value. That may be true, but that doesn't mean you don't evaluate it at all. Every business investment is measured against its ROI. If you avoid it, your executives may think you're trying to hide an underperforming program. It's time to embrace ROI measurement while you devise other measures that illustrate social media's holistic value to the organization.

---

1. 2012 Social Media Marketing Industry Report released by Social Media Examiner.

The first barrier to measuring social media that you will have to overcome to is your own perception of whether social media should be measured the same way as other marketing programs.

Standards Are the Problem

The other issue you've likely experienced is that the industry has not adopted a standard for social media measurement. Every company has its own measure of success, and sometimes even that changes from one social media campaign to the next. That makes it especially challenging to persuade your executives that the success measures you're using are the right ones. This is clouded even further by the reports that are presented to executives. Look at your last executive social media report. Were the metrics you presented manager-level metrics or executive-level metrics? Executives are overwhelmed when their marketing teams try to train them on new metrics instead of correlating the metrics with things executives care about: sales volume, revenue, and cost.

Use those core business metrics, and figure out how your social media metrics align with them in your organization. This will allow you to finally have an apples-to-apples comparison across marketing channels.

Confusion Between Measurement and Monitoring Tools Is the Problem

Measuring tools, monitoring tools, and engagement tools are very different things. To put this in perspective, consider how you manage your website: You have a content management system that allows you to publish content. Maybe you use Google Alerts so you're notified when your brand is mentioned on third-party websites. And maybe you use Google Analytics to produce reports on how your website is performing. In the social media software space are tools that essentially allow the same level of control over social media channels. Perhaps you use HootSuite to schedule and publish your status updates; this is your social media engagement console. It's where you engage with your fans and followers. You may use Radian6 or Sysomos listening tools to monitor social conversations related to your brand and your industry. These tools scour the Web to find conversations that are relevant and produce results that occur on social networks, blogs, forums, discussion boards, and other networks that HootSuite doesn't search. When these tools find a relevant conversation, they allow you to engage with the poster and respond. There is some overlap among those three tools, but each has certain features that are better than the others. Last, you may have connected your HootSuite account to Google Analytics so you can track social traffic to your website.

None of these tools gives you end-to-end measurement. The only tool that offers anything close is Google Analytics, but even that requires some work to understand. This confusion has led to frustrated social media management software customers who are dissatisfied with the reports their new measurement tool generates. How did this happen? Marketing. Almost all the software packages make marketing claims that they can measure ROI. Some claim to be an end-to-end or all-in-one solution. Because marketers are looking for a shiny software box to solve the measurement problems, they believe.

To calculate ROI you need to be able to connect the investment in social media to the revenue generated. That provides two critical pieces to calculate social media ROI; what you've spent and the sales that resulted. Therefore, a tool can measure ROI only if it actually connects to the software system that tracks revenue; for most companies, that is their CRM system. Just because some of the software providers connect to a CRM system doesn't mean they can actually track what needs to be tracked to produce the reports you want. The investment piece is the easy part; we know what we've spent, and we can back in those numbers. A tool also needs to track customers who have engaged in the social channel. You'll have to do some homework to find the right solution. Many times this involves a monitoring tool, an engagement tool, and a measurement tool. Unfortunately, today those may come in separate packages with different providers.

Lack of Maturity in Measurement Tools Is the Problem

Social media measurement tools are in their infancy. If you compare the metrics offered within these tools with the metrics that have been discussed previously, it's clear they have focused on manager-level metrics that help you know whether you're making progress. The data they provide is important, but it fails to paint the picture that helps tell the story for executives.

People expect a social media measurement tool to provide the answers, but social media is only one piece in the path to conversion. Add in the confusion about what social media really is, and it's even tougher to measure. What networks should be included in a measurement platform? Twitter, Facebook, and LinkedIn for sure. But what about your blog, forums, message boards, YouTube, Tumblr, Pinterest, and mobile campaigns? Where does social begin and end? If social media contacts wind up converting in traditional channels like email, should email data be integrated? The social media industry has expanded so quickly that, even with unlimited resources, it would be difficult to build the perfect measurement tool. Many measurement software companies have opted to specialize in data that is segmented to address the needs of their niche or target audiences. The infancy of the industry isn't an excuse for avoiding measurement altogether. It requires a little bit of effort, but the data is there if you know where to look and how to roll it into a presentable format.

Social Media Silos Are the Problem

Social media adoption in organizations is taking on many shapes and sizes. Some companies don't have full-fledged "social media teams," but they have given social media responsibility to their marketing, communications, or public relations departments. These teams have the best opportunity to see the big picture of where social media fits in the organization and where it is helping the rest of their efforts. But that isn't happening as often as it should. Instead, social media is being held up as a special marketing channel that has totally unique needs and effects on the organization. That's malarkey. And worse, it's walling social media into a silo and dramatically limiting its potential. Further, when there are separate departments, territory issues start to arise. It's Corporate Politics 101. Even the best-intentioned social media teams wind up battling with other marketing teams over "your projects" and "our projects." This can further isolate social media and make it even more difficult to develop strategies that work across multiple marketing channels.

The nature of social media lends itself to cross-department integration, but it's taking time for companies to come to terms with that. This certainly isn't the case for all organizations, but plenty of people reading this are shaking their heads right now. It's a tough challenge. On one hand, companies don't want anyone with a keyboard and an Internet connection having access to the corporate social media channels. Putting control of social media in the wrong hands can turn into mayhem that's a risk to the organization. On the other hand, companies can't keep social media locked in a box that only the people "who get it" are allowed to touch. That walls out people who are excited about social media and have value to bring to the table. This conundrum will take time to work out and most likely will be solved with a balanced approach. In the meantime, social media is sitting out there by itself.

From a measurement perspective, this is an even bigger problem. For many companies, social media metrics alone aren't that impressive, especially in the building stage of adoption. Executives would look at most social media data and call it a miserable failure. This is because the organization's approach to it hasn't had time to mature. Social media hasn't been optimized like the other marketing channels; just imagine how long it took for companies to get pay-per-click advertising right. There was a lot of trial and error, and that's where most marketers are with social media. It's in the trial-and-error phase, yet marketers are being asked to present data that assumes they have the formula for success figured out.

This is why it's crucial to stop measuring social media in a silo. Social media data will be able to stand on its own two feet eventually, but even then looking at the data in isolation leaves out important parts of the story. Instead, compare social media data across marketing channels. This will show how social media is helping to lower the costs and improve the results of other marketing initiatives. The channels for presenting combined information will vary based on whether you're focused on brand awareness, lead generation, or customer retention, but the following list is a good start.

Present social media alongside these marketing channels:

- Online advertising (PPC, display, remarketing)
- Offline advertising (TV, radio, print)
- Search engine optimization
- Public relations
- Events
- Direct mail
- Email marketing

> *This is why it's crucial to stop measuring social media in a silo. Social media data will be able to stand on its own two feet eventually, but even then looking at the data in isolation leaves out important parts of the story.*

This list is also a great starting point for figuring out if there's an opportunity to integrate social media elements into any of the other areas' efforts. The challenge may be figuring out how to show social media's involvement with these channels in a meaningful way. The data from the social media channel may not flow into the reporting dashboards that are used for these marketing channels. You may need to create your own dashboard and align them the best you can.

The Path to Conversion Is the Problem

Social media has amplified one major challenge with tracking marketing: how to give credit to all touch points throughout the campaign history. Tools like Google Analytics credit the last campaign registered before conversion. This often short-changes social media because the social media interaction can be earlier in the sales process. To solve this problem, Google released its "social reports" feature, which begins to show how many "assists" were generated from social media. This essentially shows how many conversions touched the social media channel and then converted through another campaign. But this still doesn't tell the story that you're looking for.

Marketers want to understand *every* marketing campaign that contributed to a sale, and not just to get credit for it. Frankly, many marketers wouldn't care who got credit if they just understood what the true campaign history looked like because then they would be able to show hard data on their role in the conversion process. That information would be invaluable for optimizing their results. Imagine them realizing that when a lead comes from the social channel to the blog and then downloads an e-book and clicks on a pay-per-click advertisement later, conversion is 200% better. Do you think they might build a remarketing program in Google to try to scale those results? Absolutely. It's certainly worth a test.

This capability exists only in pieces. Some marketers can get partial data from their marketing automation package, other pieces from Google Analytics, and other pieces through their CRM. Other marketers can't get more than what Google Analytics offers. The power of full campaign history is game-changing, and it can't happen fast enough. This isn't a social media tracking problem; it's a universal marketing problem. Creating a campaign history table that tracks web and cross-channel marketing response activity that's tied to a unique user would solve it, but the industry isn't quite there yet. Marketing automation packages give the deepest level of insight into the path to conversion, but getting the data out in a meaningful way isn't always easy.

Your Systems Are the Problem

The systems your organization is using to collect data may be preventing you from getting the data you need. Think about all the software packages marketing uses to deploy campaigns and initiatives. The list is probably long. This is a sampling of the software systems a midsize organization might use. When you get into large enterprise organizations, the list grows substantially.

Website	Advertising	PR	Social Media	Email	CRM/Accounting
WordPress	AdWords	Cision	HootSuite	ExactTarget	Salesforce CRM
Google Analytics	AdSense	Burrells Luce	Raven tools		FinancialForce invoicing
Omniture	Advertising.com		Facebook Insights		

Website	Advertising	PR	Social Media	Email	CRM/Accounting
	Marketron (Radio)				
	Google TV ads		YouTube Insights		

How many of those systems can pass data back and forth? Is there one place to get a holistic view of the data from each of these systems? The answer is likely no. Although adding software packages helps solve your short-term data needs, it may make the holistic picture harder to come by. Most software companies will tell you they have an application programming interface, or API. API is a fancy term that means they have opened their programming code for integration with other systems or custom programming. And many of them do have an API. But few companies that buy the software go on to create a single view of the data from all their software packages because of what it costs to actually integrate them. The other challenge is that marketers are taking a bird's-eye view. They figure out how many followers they have, see growth, and are happy. But the on-the-ground view is most important: How many of those followers are customers, how many are prospects, how many are influencers, and how many are media contacts? Marketers need to understand how many of those followers are email subscribers, how many have visited the website, and how many responded to that last campaign.

That bird's-eye data is important, but the data that is going to help marketers succeed is deep within the customer record. They need to be able to tie actions back to an individual and then aggregate that data to spot trends that are not only insightful, but actionable. That requires systems to talk to each other. Stop and think before adding yet another shiny new social media software package. Instead, focus on connecting the systems you have. Concentrate on mining those tools to find integration points that will start tying in your social media data and make it meaningful to the front office.

Don't Stop Now

This doesn't mean stop everything. Some simple solutions could work wonders. Susan Kim has a great philosophy for this: "Progress before perfection." No, all the issues can't be solved right now, but fixing a few little things will mean faster progress toward better data. The important thing is to keep the goal in sight, or two years from now you'll still be struggling to piece together data from multiple reports and trying to make something meaningful out of it. The following exercise will help identify opportunities to get better, more meaningful data.

Hands-On Exercise: Finding and Overcoming Your Barriers

One of the largest challenges you'll face is tracking those who touch the social media channel through the entire path to conversion. The first step in solving this problem is to understand what the path to conversion might look like. In most organizations, there could be a thousand combinations of how prospective customers could come into the organization and a thousand other combinations for marketing channels they could touch after they're customers. Because of the high variability in the linear path to conversion, this exercise brings clarity to the multiple possible touch points. The next chapter helps you find ways to begin connecting the dots to create a measureable path.

In the following table, list all the marketing communications vehicles a prospect could touch during the path to conversion into a customer. In the first column, create a list of marketing communications content. In the second column, write down the action the prospect would take that could produce a measureable result. Finally, in the third column list where that data is currently stored. There are a few samples to help you get started.

The purpose of this exercise is to help you get a handle on the variety of actions a prospect can take and where the data lives within the organization. This will give you the framework you need to complete the exercises in the following chapter. If you're focused on a customer retention strategy, the worksheets you will need follow the prospect worksheets. You will go through the same steps, but you'll focus on actions a customer could take throughout the customer life cycle.

Prospect Marketing Audit		
Marketing Content	**Trackable Action**	**Where Data Is Stored**
Tweet	Link click	Bit.ly
PPC ad	Link click	AdWords Dashboard
Organic search listing	Link click	Google Analytics
Email campaign	Link click	ExactTarget

Prospect Marketing Audit *(continued)*		
Marketing Content	Trackable Action	Where Data Is Stored

Customer Marketing Audit		
Marketing Content	Trackable Action	Where Data Is Stored
Email newsletter	Sales offer	ExactTarget, Salesforce
Customer email campaign	Sales offer	ExactTarget, Salesforce
Facebook status update	Link clicked	Facebook Insights, Bit.ly

Customer Marketing Audit *(continued)*		
Marketing Content	**Trackable Action**	**Where Data Is Stored**

10

Understanding the Dots That Need to Connect to Facilitate End-to-End Measurement

As you saw in Chapter 9, "Breaking Down the Barriers to Social Media Measurement," the barriers to measurement run deep. They open conversations that are much bigger than how to measure social media because they affect the way marketing campaigns are tracked throughout the entire company. This creates opportunities, but it can also create turf wars among departments that want to hold onto "credit." Departments may feel that tracking full campaign history will dilute their numbers and make it tougher to meet their goals. Even if they have been allies, departments could become enemies if they think you're trying to turn their reporting system upside down.

So don't make tracking full campaign history about "credit." Instead, position the need in terms of the ability to optimize everyone's success. Having a full campaign history paints a more realistic picture of the true cost per lead and the true cost of customer retention. Even though your executive team is desperate for this information, the rest of the departments may argue over whether this is the right thing to do. That's because it may make for short-term undesirable results, while it's on its way to eventual positive impact. Instead, focus on that eventuality—the intended outcome that will help all marketing areas understand how they can deliver better results. Once you have the data and have been able to use it to increase success, you can broach the subject of how comprehensive reporting is presented and analyzed.

But first you need to figure out how this is even possible. This chapter is designed to help you track full campaign history for prospects and customers. (*Full campaign history* means that you have the ability to see every action that a prospect or customer has taken before, during, and after a revenue-generating activity.) Full campaign history is bigger than the immediate actions before, during, and after the action that drove revenue. It tracks data over the entire life cycle of the lead and customer, which lets you see trends that happen over time and even lets you move toward predictive analysis. Furthermore, predictive analysis allows you to see if you can re-create those trends, using that data to plan future marketing efforts for implementation at just the right times. That's the long-term vision of why campaign history is important. In the short term, it shows how long it takes to convert leads that came through the social channel and which path to conversion delivers the highest conversion rates. For customer retention strategies, this helps you figure out where social media is most important in the life cycle of the customer and identify what generates the highest retention rate and customer lifetime value.

> *The million-dollar question is, "What dots do you need to connect to truly measure social media?"*

Why Full Campaign History Is Important

You've heard the adage that half of your marketing budget is wasted; you just aren't sure which half. This realization might paralyze you as a marketer. You might think you can't stop anything because you might remove the thing that was working. It doesn't help that the impact of marketing changes may take months or even years to play out because of the life cycle of your customers. Even social media marketers aren't out there telling companies to stop their other marketing activities to dump their budgets into social media because social media results are still fairly nebulous for many organizations. Understanding full marketing campaign history solves this problem.

What Dots Need to Connect

The million-dollar question is, "What dots do you need to connect to truly measure social media?" First, however, you need to know what all the dots are—what touch points a prospect or customer makes on the path to conversion. The hands-on exercise in Chapter 9 identified these actions and showed where the data about them is stored. One element in most marketing channels is the cornerstone of the call to action: the URL. In social media, people share links to their latest blog post, their latest video, and other types of resources. In email marketing, people provide links to articles or promotions. Also making a presence in outdoor, print, and even TV advertising are QR codes that use URLs to drive to landing pages. Marketers put URLs in everything, but they fail to ensure that URL tracking is integrated into other reporting systems. The best way to figure out the dots you need to connect is to look at how a URL is tracked through your organization's tracking systems. Just using a centralized process for creating links could provide a tremendous level of insight. Figure 10.1 provides a short overview of how links are created and where data is stored through three marketing channels.

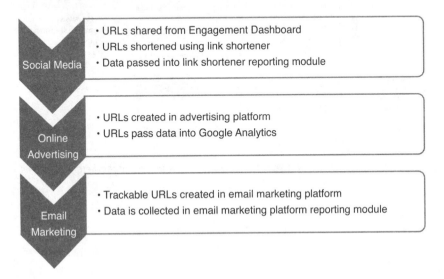

Figure 10.1 *URLs provide an opportunity for integrated data.*

The best example of tracking from these three systems is found in online advertising. The online advertising URL framework is mature, and because online ads typically drive to a landing page on a company's website, the data already tracks into website analytics packages. Clearly, the URL is a dot that needs to connect through these systems. Think about how you share content in the social channel and what your path to conversion might look like. Figure 10.2 provides a basic sample of what a Twitter follower might go through to become a customer. As you can see, three systems hold data related to the customer. Because the prospect became a customer in this example, there would also be data in the customer relationship management (CRM). But does your CRM know that the customer originated from Twitter? Probably not. Review the list you made in the exercise from Chapter 9. Which calls to action appear over and over again? How much knowledge would you have if you could integrate that data point across all your platforms? Figure 10.3 provides a starter list of systems that a prospect and customer could touch in your organization and that you can review for integration potential. Remember, your goal is to get the campaign history into the CRM, and the best way to do that is through a trackable URL, so think about the best way to connect URL data into the CRM system. I'm going to show you one way to do just that.

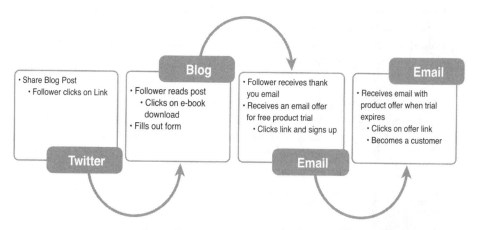

Figure 10.2   *Social media users can interact with a variety of marketing channels.*

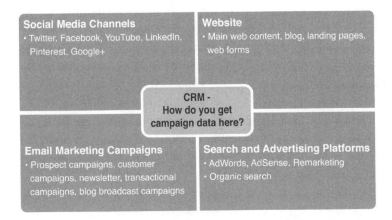

Social Media Channels	Website
• Twitter, Facebook, YouTube, LinkedIn, Pinterest, Google+	• Main web content, blog, landing pages, web forms

**CRM -
How do you get
campaign data here?**

Email Marketing Campaigns	Search and Advertising Platforms
• Prospect campaigns, customer campaigns, newsletter, transactional campaigns, blog broadcast campaigns	• AdWords, AdSense, Remarketing • Organic search

Figure 10.3 *The CRM is at the center of prospect and customer touch points.*

Is Getting Full Campaign History into Your CRM System Really Possible?

The first question you probably have is, "Is this even possible?" The answer is yes. And it may not be as difficult as it sounds. Now that it's clear that the big common denominator in the digital channel is the URL, there's a huge opportunity for integration that can act as a starting point. Remember, progress comes before perfection.

The first step is tracking URLs that drive to your own web properties and determining whether those URLs will enable you to understand users' downstream activity.

The second step is being able to track URLs that drive to third-party websites. This is especially important to social media. In most advertising channels, you drive every user to a website the company owns. But a big part of social media is sharing resources that others publish. The most successful companies share others' resources more than they share their own; sometimes as much as 80% of shared content comes from third-party publishers. The big question is, when you share a link to a third-party website, does the person who goes there ever come back to *your* website? And if he does, what does he do then? This huge gap in the data could tell an important story for social media practitioners. Although there isn't a simple, out-of-a-box solution to this problem, there are options.

Finding Opportunities for Integration

One thing that helps is being able to better track URLs that drive to your own web properties. Google has made great strides in this by allowing marketers to tag their websites with Urchin Traffic Monitor (UTM) parameters that are recognized within Google Analytics and pass through their reporting (see Figure 10.4). Technically, these UTM fields are added to the end of the URL, and Google Analytics looks for them when someone visits the site. A cookie is placed on the visitor's computer, and when the visitor completes a goal that is set up in Google Analytics, it reads the cookie and passes the campaign fields into Google Analytics.

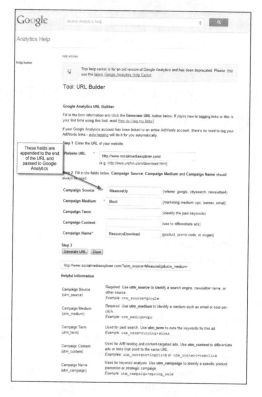

Figure 10.4 *Google's URL builder appends campaign parameters to URLs.*

The URL that Google generated in the example in Figure 10.4 looks like this: http://www.socialmediaexplorer.com/?utm_source=MeasureUp&utm_medium=Book&utm_campaign=ResourceDownload. You can see where the fields MeasureUp, Book, and ResourceDownload were added in the URL. This technology is already used for search engine optimization (SEO) and all online advertising that runs through a Google advertising engine. If you had used the

UTM parameters of Twitter, Status Update, and March, you would be able to find information shown in Figure 10.5 inside your Google Analytics dashboard under Campaign.

Figure 10.5 *How UTM parameters appear in Google Analytics*

To get the level of data shown in Figure 10.5, you need to have goals set up in Google Analytics. This means you can use a reporting system you already have to get better insights for your social media campaigns. (Yes, it makes for long URLs. Resist the urge to shorten them, though, because doing so eliminates the tracking function that gets the data you need.) This gets even easier if you use HootSuite as your engagement platform; it has a direct integration with Google Analytics, so you can add the UTM parameters right within the dashboard. This is important because most SEO and online advertising teams also use the Google framework, and now you are all using the same system. That's progress, and it's something you can do today.

Google also laid the groundwork for solving part of the problem with tracking campaign history with its Social Reports feature. Right now, social media may be bringing opportunities to the table, but those opportunities become customers through other online marketing activities. When social media is a top-of-funnel contributor like that, its conversion data probably looks lackluster. The Social Reports feature changes that. It identifies the "social media assist" and proves that social media is a contributor to the bottom line, as shown in Figure 10.6.

Another part of the equation is connecting the dots from third-party websites. What happens to people you send there? The philosophy that sharing content from others will build trust with your audience hasn't been backed up with hard data. Are prospects really more likely to convert if they visit a third-party resource you shared? There is only one way to find out, and getting there takes a little bit of custom development. When you send people to a third-party site, you need to intercept them before they get there and put your tracking parameters in place. The best way to do that is to build a custom URL shortener that intercepts this process and drops in the tracking code before they get to the third-party site. Then you need to store the data so your web analytics package can read it. The easiest way is to append Google's custom URL parameters before the link is shortened.

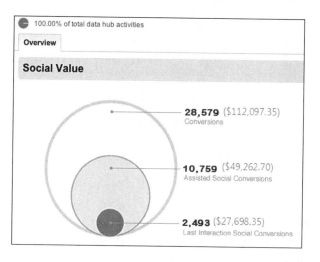

Figure 10.6   *Google's Social Reports track social media assists.*

Chapter 12, "A Great Starter Mix of Tools for Less Than $10 a Month," will show you a system to apply Google's custom parameters to URLs when you share them in the social channel. That insight will give you more data than you've ever had, and it will be a tremendous step toward optimizing your success. That's progress. However, it's equally important to recognize where the gaps are so that you can jump on opportunities to fill them. The rest of the chapter helps you understand the big picture so you don't miss any simple integrations, like the one with Google Analytics.

Conducting a System Audit

To get anywhere close to fixing the problem of tracking campaign history, you need to have a better understanding of what software systems and tools you're already using. A system audit gets you there. This kind of audit helps organizations of any size understand what tools are being used, but small companies aren't likely to have resources to do any custom integrating of those tools. For midsize and enterprise organizations, this is best handled with the help of your best software engineers. They will understand what points of integration are possible.

The first step is to find what systems are in place for your CRM, web analytics, campaign tracking, marketing automation, email campaigns, social media monitoring, social media engagement, and social media measurement, just to list a few. To tackle that beast, list each department or area of responsibility: customer service, sales, public relations, marketing, communications, and advertising. Then go to each department and ask what systems it is using. You may find that several departments are using the same systems. That's good because it shows opportunity for high-value integration of your data. Another good place to find out which systems are in place is to ask your Information Technology (IT) department. They will have an understanding of the systems in use and the application programming interface (API) opportunities that exist to connect data. Then identify which programming languages the software systems use, and find out whether there's an API available to help them communicate. For small companies, this may require a phone call to the software vendor. (Note: Not all APIs are created equal. Just because one exists doesn't mean integration will be a breeze.)

Next, you need to find out if you have any kind of data warehouse that's being used to mash up data and if there is a reporting system in place. Sometimes this is a MySQL database that pulls data from multiple systems and pushes it to something like Crystal Reports to present the data in a meaningful way. This is more common in larger organizations that have large amounts of data to be mined.

Prioritizing Data Initiatives

When you understand what the systems are and have a good handle on potential integration points, it's time to look for low-effort, high-value opportunities. Start to identify how to pass data among the existing systems, rather than creating a whole new social media system and process. Look for small opportunities to begin integrating your data. Hint: Become really good friends with that super-smart software engineer.

For example, if you use Google's campaign tracking system for online advertising, you can apply the same custom URL parameters for social media links and pass your data into Google Analytics through HootSuite or Argyle Social (see Figure 10.7). Ask your software engineer for a level of effort, or LOE, for passing social media data into any system that connects with the CRM system. And ask for the LOE for going straight to the CRM system. Rank the list of systems in terms of priority for integration. Start with the systems that get you closest to having full campaign history and a connection to an individual account record. Here's the good news. If you have a marketing automation system in place, you will find that you have a robust data set for online campaign history, but there may be a gap for tracking UTM campaign parameters from social media links. That may be an easy problem to fix once you talk with your IT representative.

Figure 10.7 shows the type of opportunities you're looking for.

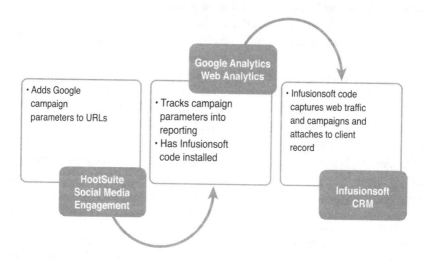

Figure 10.7 *This example shows potential opportunities for passing data into the CRM.*

The bad news is that full integration will take time and resources. The good news is that a variety of systems integrate already or have plug-ins that quickly connect them without a lot of effort and development expense. Focus on those options first and put the rest on the back burner.

It would be very wise to get your IT department involved early. You should tell them that you are trying to understand the current systems that are being used to track marketing activities so you can see if there is a way to easily integrate social media data. They will have a better understanding of what is and isn't easy to do and can explain what their current priorities are. If you don't have an IT department, you may have to hire external resources to assist with a full integration effort. However, you may get push back because your management team will want to see that the investment will pay off. It's the typical chicken and egg scenario. Your boss wants to see the return first, but you need the resources to be able to accurately track the return. If you find yourself in this situation, focus on the data you can get easily to begin showing progress. Once you have enough data to show a positive impact, it will be easier to justify the resources you'll need to be able to employ end-to-end tracking.

Hands-On Exercise: Systems Audit

The best way to get a handle on your barriers to data collection is to understand where data is being stored and how it passes from one system to another. This exercise helps you identify key systems capable of holding data that is important to your social media strategy and identify opportunities to pass data from one system to another. Your ultimate goal is to get your social media and website data attached to a client record in your CRM system.

Use the following questionnaire for each department in your organization:

1. What software packages are you using?

2. Do any of those packages collect customer data?

3. Do any of those packages pass data to the CRM? If so, how? What data do they pass? Where is the data stored inside the CRM?

4. Do any of the software packages you're using collect marketing data like campaign names or lead sources? If so, which one? What marketing information is being collected? Where is it being stored? Is it being passed into the CRM?

5. For any software package that you answered yes for questions 3 or 4: Does this software package have an API? What language is it programmed in? What type of database (for example, MySQL) is used? Do you know if there is an integration with (name of CRM)? Do you know someone I could contact to find out?

After you find systems that have potential integration points with social media data, see which system has the most integrations across the board. Also see if any systems that you know already are connected and can get you to the CRM, even if it's in a roundabout way.

System Audit Worksheet

Use Figure 10.8 to write down the software packages used by each department. If you see the same software package being used in multiple areas, circle it!

Finding Integration Opportunities

Does a software package stand out because it's frequently listed? Do any of the packages that already integrate with your CRM offer the opportunity to pass social media data? You will start with the URL you share on a social media channel and track back how you will get the data into your web analytics package and your CRM. You will need someone who has technical expertise to help you with this section. Write down your thoughts on the possible systems that you could use to make the connections in Figure 10.9.

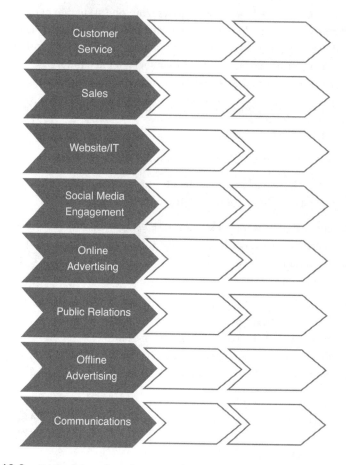

Figure 10.8 *Write down the software packages that are being used in each area of responsibility.*

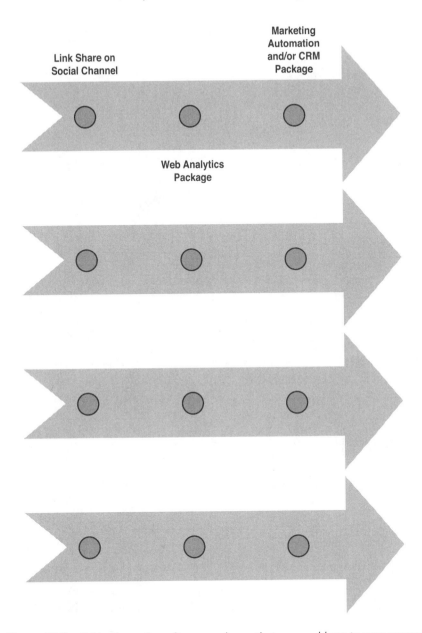

Figure 10.9 *Write down the software packages that you could use to pass campaign data from one channel to the next.*

11

Measurement Tool Review

To implement the recommendations in this book, you need a software solution to get to the data you want. You may find that your existing tools give you some or most of the data you need. If that's the case, congratulations! You are ahead of the game. But for most, implementing the recommendations requires bringing some new tools into the mix.

For the purpose of this exercise, monitoring tools are defined as platforms for scanning social media networks and websites for key words and phrases that are relevant to the organization. Engagement tools are platforms for publishing and replying to status updates within the interface. They also may include workflow tools, like the ability to assign posts to other users for reply. Measurement tools are platforms for tracking the success of your social media efforts that tie into conversions and provide reporting. More than 25 tools were reviewed, and 5 were selected based on their ability to measure results that tie into conversion tracking and cross-channel analysis from the social channel. There are plenty of monitoring and engagement tools that aren't reviewed because they don't provide the level of sophistication in measurement that aligns with the methodologies presented throughout the rest of the book, but that doesn't mean they aren't perfectly good monitoring and engagement tools. Tools like Core Metrics and Omniture can, in theory, track many of the metrics described throughout this section, but the cost of implementing them and customizing them may make them unrealistic for many organizations, so they were excluded.

The social media industry has focused heavily on building best-in-breed social media management systems for the past several years, but recently more sophistication has popped up around measuring ROI as marketers have started demanding it. This focus on measurement has inspired a few social media management systems to build up their measurement capabilities, but it has also created a whole suite of tools specifically for measurement. The tools reviewed here were selected for their measurement capability. A few of them have monitoring and engagement features, and that is included in the review. That said, the rating system is based solely upon measurement capability. Each review contains the same categories to provide an apples-to-apples comparison. The order of these reviews is not an indication of the quality of the tool, but an alphabetical sort.

Argyle Social Review

Cost—$400–$1,100 per month*

Classification—Engagement and Measurement

Overall Rating—3 stars

Website—http://www.argylesocial.com

"Argyle Social helps businesses drive results through social media. We provide software to help your organization participate in conversations with prospects and customers, drive brand awareness, and integrate social media deeply throughout your organization. And behind the scenes, we crunch your social activity through our big data engine to provide you with the most actionable social intelligence in the business."

*Argyle has an entry-level license for $300 per month; however, it lacks conversion reporting, which is a key feature for data analysis.

Overview

Argyle Social provides a social media publishing, engagement, and measurement platform. The goal for this tool was to provide best-in-class measurement of the social channel while allowing marketers to easily manage their presence in the same platform. Overall, this is a strong engagement platform that integrates several key measurement features for marketers.

Included are basic monitoring features of Twitter, Facebook, and Google+. The solid engagement platform allows marketers to quickly publish and engage in their social channels, as shown in Figure 11.1. The interface is reminiscent of TweetDeck, which provides a level of familiarity to users. One great feature is the ability to post variations of a status update to multiple networks in one dashboard. Each of the links assigned to the status updates automatically tracks separately based on the social network where the content was posted. This helps marketers optimize their efforts because they know exactly which status update and which channel drove conversions.

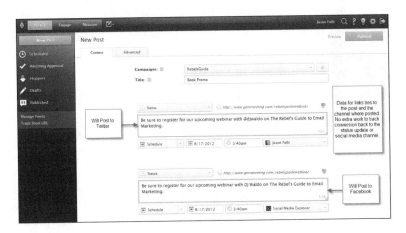

Figure 11.1   *Argyle Social provides a solid publishing, engagement, and measurement platform.*

There's also a feature, similar to Buffr, that allows marketers to put several updates in what they call a *Hopper*. The Hopper will spread these updates throughout the day at pre-defined times without requiring the user to manually schedule the time they will publish. This is great for marketers who review a mass amount of content from blogs and other sources at a specific time of the day but don't want to inundate their social streams and share the content all at once. Argyle also has a standard set of workflow features that allow marketers to assign posts, review assigned posts, and even include approval workflows for publishing new content. Argyle also offers a solid publishing and engagement platform that could easily be used as a marketer's primary daily engagement solution.

Overall Measurement Features (3.7 Stars)

Argyle provides a solid base for measuring social media conversions as shown in Figure 11.2, but it still has some work to do to truly take social media measurement to the next level.

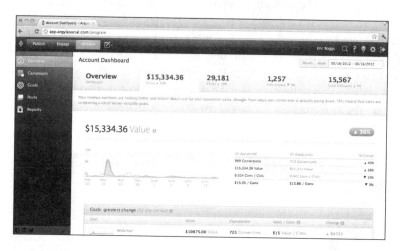

Figure 11.2 *Argyle provides a quick snapshot analysis of campaigns.*

Third-Party Integrations (2 Stars)

The tool allows marketers to track results either through integration with Google Analytics or by means of Argyle's proprietary tracking system that adds a few extras to Google Analytics's methodology. However, only conversions from Argyle's proprietary tracking system will show up. Google Analytics users will need to log in to their Google Analytics account to see conversion data.

Social Media Data Tracking (5 Stars)

Argyle does a great job at pulling social media stats, such as growth in fans and fol-lowers, number of mentions, comments, and others, into their system. All the basic social media data points are tracked with this system. It's the data most tools use to claim they are a measurement tool, but Argyle recognizes that conversion is one of the most important elements.

Conversion Tracking (4 Stars)

Argyle's measurement system is built on tracking links in status updates to con-versions—a solid philosophy. The system is built around utilizing campaigns to associate multiple status updates with an overall campaign. Within the interface, you can add revenue values for goals, which is strongly recommended. You've already heard about the risks associated with tracking fake revenue. But Argyle knew that wasn't going to cut it and released an integration with Salesforce to pass campaign data to the contact record. That's a big deal and sets Argyle apart from the competition. Now it's possible to associate website conversions with real revenue, even for companies that do not sell their product or service online— something none of the other tools is able to do.

Argyle built much of its early messaging based on its attribution model, which allows you to track any conversion that social media played a role in compared to other systems that only credit social media when it was the last touch prior to a conversion. A similar feature has since been released within Google Analytics as well. Argyle does a good job of integrating measurement requirements into the engagement workflow and passing the data into the reporting portal. It's a solid system for marketers who lack any kind of social media conversion reporting.

The only downside is that you have to install code on your conversion pages for conversions to report through Argyle. The system doesn't pull in conversions tracked through Google Analytics. For some marketers, this will present a minor barrier to getting tracking up and running. For those with complicated policies around website changes, this could be a deal-breaker.

Reporting Features (2 Stars)

The reporting dashboard offers an overview of the revenue value, clicks, interactions and changes in followers for the time period selected compared to the previous period, as shown in Figure 11.3. This shows at a glance whether activities are up or down over the prior period.

Figure 11.3 *Argyle's quick overview reporting*

Conversion Reporting (2 Stars)

Argyle allows you to drill down to see all the performance for each post associated with a campaign and even top performing goals so you can quickly analyze what is over- or underperforming. This speeds up optimization for marketers trying to figure out which goal is performing the best or worst.

However, Argyle reports all conversions using the term *social value*, indicating that social media was involved in the conversion. It does not display where social media contributed to the conversion in the process or provide insight into how its attribution model credits a conversion. This is a challenge because marketers want to understand whether it was a social media assist or a true social media conversion. You won't be able to identify how conversions break down into these two categories.

By clicking on a goal, you can see all the posts and URLs that drove conversion. However, conversion tracking is limited to conversions that are tracked through Argyle's proprietary system. The reporting interface will not pull data from third-party integrations like Google Analytics. This is unfortunate because it means you'll likely still get a lot of your cross-channel data out of Google Analytics or your web analytics tool. Cross-channel comparison is so important to demonstrating social media's real value.

Summary Report Features (4 Stars)

The summary dashboard provides the highest level of data for reporting; however, there is no clear option to download data displayed on the dashboard or schedule reports using the data from the interface. You can download the Twitter and Facebook reports, but the summary report would be more useful. This makes it difficult for marketers to use the data for presentations to management teams without taking multiple screen shots.

Report Export and Customization (2 Stars)

The Reports tab lists two reports that you can pull: Twitter and Facebook. You can build some custom reports for download; however, the feature was a little clunky and difficult to use. The help system didn't provide instructions, and the feature to build a custom report couldn't be found, but it is a feature that is offered.

Argyle also offers the ability to create white-label reports for agencies. The ability to build customized reports could be far more intuitive. Overall, the reporting suite had all of the features most users would want, but it will need a user interface overhaul to make it easy for marketers to get the data they need quickly.

Data Presentation (2 Stars)

The data that is presented through Argyle offers drill-down insight for marketers; however, the presentation is limited to data collected through Argyle. It doesn't allow marketers to add data points such as budgets for campaigns, which would allow for calculations such as cost per impression, cost per engagement, and cost per conversion. This requires marketers to create their own dashboard to calculate the data points discussed throughout the book. The big limitation is not being able to do cross-channel analysis and provide data from channels outside of social media. However, marketers using Salesforce may be able to tie this together by pulling reports out of Salesforce.

Expion

> **Cost**—$1,500–$2,500 per month for brands plus $25–$50 per month per location for multiunit management. Setup fees start at $200.
>
> **Classification**—Monitoring, Engagement, and Measurement
>
> **Overall Rating**—3.8 stars
>
> **Website**—http://www.expion.com
>
> "Expion is a social software company. Our centralized platform empowers global brands, agencies, and retailers to localize and manage their social marketing efforts. Expion provides scalable enterprise-grade software to listen, content plan, publish, moderate, analyze, govern, and share content on Facebook and other social channels across thousands of users. The system produces real-time community intelligence giving brands and retailers the power to optimize consumer engagement, service, and ad performance."
>
> Expion is a tool specifically designed to manage multiple brands under an umbrella or thousands of locations in a franchise or retail system.

Overview

Expion provides a social media monitoring, publishing, engagement, and measurement platform, as shown in Figure 11.4. It is specifically focused on companies managing hundreds of brands and franchise organizations that have thousands of locations to manage. Its goal is to provide brand customization and localization in a scalable and manageable interface for multiple user access levels.

Figure 11.4   *Expion provides intense monitoring, engagement, and data analysis for global brands and multiunit marketers.*

Expion's robust monitoring across social and web channels is on par with Radian6 and Sysomos. However, it also includes in-depth monitoring of review sites such as Yelp, Google Places, and others. This is clearly an important piece for Expion's audience. Its publishing platform is built for handling the complications of managing hundreds or even thousands of brands. It allows marketers to create approved libraries of status updates, schedule updates across multiple locations quickly, and even combine features similar to a mail merge field that allows the same status update to be localized automatically.

One of Expion's key differentiators is its ability to spawn links that are created through its system. This means when you post the same link in a status update that will be published to 1,000 locations, its system actually creates 1,000 unique URLs that can be individually tracked. This feature is powerful for analyzing independent locations and rolling data into regional and system-level reports.

Expion provides a best-in-class tool for large-scale social media management and publishing. Now it is adding a robust measurement platform that will make it a force to be reckoned with.

Overall Measurement Features (3.6 Stars)

When it comes to measuring across multiple brands or thousands of locations, Expion is in a league of its own. Imagine the complexity of aggregating data that is published onto thousands of social profiles; however, it has built a system that makes this easy and provides drill-down and roll-up reporting quickly. Imagine the power of being able to track that one store is outperforming all others in the sale of a product and then being able to drill down into its social profiles to find out why. You could leverage that knowledge across all other locations or even save the high-performing status updates into a library so that other locations could follow suit. For consumer brands like Procter & Gamble, which has thousands of subbrands, this capability allows brand managers to easily produce brand-level reporting, but it also allows for cross-brand analysis to see how the overall Procter & Gamble portfolio is performing or how segments of its brands are reporting. This is powerful, executive-level data that is extremely hard to come by in other systems.

Third-Party Integrations (1 Star)

At the time of this review, Expion didn't have any third-party integrations for data analysis; however, this capability is high on the list for its development team.

Social Media Data Tracking (5 Stars)

Expion provides a wide range of basic social media statistics that are aggregated to the system level and can be drilled down to a location or brand level. It uses a grid system that allows marketers to create the metrics they want and break them down into segments to see how each segment is performing. This includes an in-depth list of available metrics, including fans, followers, page visits, engagement, reviews, and several others. These tables can be sorted by any of the metrics and analyzed to quickly find outliers and drill down for further analysis. The grid-based reporting is great for large data sets. Although this form of data representation is necessary for these types of companies, it isn't always pretty. So, Expion is adding more graphics-based aggregations to make summary reporting easier.

Conversion Tracking (4.75 Stars)

Expion conversion tracking is built upon the framework of its spawning URL creation, which means marketers will be able to associate campaigns and conversion points at the system or brand level and the independent page level. It currently requires code to be placed on conversion pages; however, it plans to bring in conversion and goal tracking from third-party tools.

Expion uses three levels of user-created attribution that is associated with every created link:

- **Campaign**—Campaigns tie into the overall campaign the post is about.
- **Reporting tags**—These tags allow the marketer to create user-defined reporting tags that can be focused on the brands or locations represented and other subsections they select. For example, Toyota could

select the global brand and then subselect into Camry, Prius, and others.

- **Post attributes**—These attributes allow marketers to report on creative elements in the post such as post length, time of day, and type of post, such as a question, coupon, or link.

Expion automatically attaches additional attributions such as the location, language, and social profile where the post went without additional input from the marketer. This provides the highest level of attribution tracking available from any tool.

Reporting Features (3.2 Stars)

Expion doesn't mess around when it comes to reporting. Although its grid-based user interface can be hard to look at, it's extremely powerful for data analysis.

Conversion Reporting (5 Stars)

The conversion reporting in Expion is much different from other tools because of the methodology used in creating its system. First, it focuses on wanting to understand when an individual post is involved in the conversion process, even if it wasn't the point of conversion. This means it will report on the actual posts that assisted with a conversion and plan to display where the post was involved in the path to conversion most often, but it also will display when a post was the last touch before a conversion. This is far more robust than any of the other tools because it tells you the actual point in the conversion process, whereas others only show that it assisted "somewhere" in the process. This will be very helpful for marketers who are interested in finding the optimal path to conversion based on content types and social channels. It also will show posts that are associated with a specific conversion and the percentage of converters who saw the top posts.

Expion allows marketers to provide a revenue value for each conversion point. However, for most of its clients, actual revenue is tracked at each point-of-sale system, which makes it even more difficult to tie back to a social conversion. This will make it tough for Expion to tie into real revenue in the near future. Marketers can produce reports on revenue values associated with social conversions, but it will be better to use cost-based reporting and report on the cost per conversion, rather than reporting on fake revenue values.

Summary Report Features (4 Stars)

Expion has added graphic-based reporting for high-level summary reporting that makes it easy to do quick overall analysis. This helps it balance a marketer's need for the in-depth data its grid-based system provides with the need for quick-glance analysis.

Report Export and Customization (4 Stars)

Marketers can create custom reports using any of the hundreds of metrics tracked through Expion. These reports can be exported into Excel or as a PDF. It's incorporating a drag-and-drop interface for report modules that will make report customization even more powerful.

Data Presentation (3 Stars)

Expion has similar limitations to other measurement systems, in that it reports on the social channel, which doesn't allow for cross-channel reporting. However, its URL shortener allows marketers to create URLs with all the attribution reporting that can be placed in other types of marketing campaigns, such as emails and online advertising. These can be assigned attributes to identify where they are being posted. If marketers use the tool this way, it will provide a much more robust cross-channel reporting capability. However, the data will need to be tied into conversions that are tracked within web analytics, such as organic search conversions that can't be tied into this system. Most of the systems will allow marketers to create custom shortened URLs with attributions, but getting the data back out can be cumbersome. Expion makes this easier with its custom reporting capability. If it added campaign and monthly budgets for marketers, this would be even further improved to report on core business objectives in a way that could quickly produce executive-level reports. The level of complexity in the data makes producing pretty reports difficult, but Expion has made great strides toward simplifying aggregated data.

Raven Tools

Cost—$99 per month for brands, $249 per month for agencies

Classification—Monitoring, Engagement, and Measurement

Overall Rating—3.1 stars

Website—http://www.raventools.com

"Raven Internet Marketing Tools is an online platform that helps users quickly research, manage, monitor, and report on search engine optimization (SEO), social media, and other Internet marketing campaigns. Its collaborative, multi-user features and fast, professional reports make it the software choice of thousands of online marketers worldwide. Raven Internet Marketing Tools, a privately held Nashville-based company, was founded in 2007."

Overview

Raven offers a great tool for small to midsize businesses and agencies that combines the power of an engagement and monitoring tool with robust analytics from a variety of sources, as shown in Figure 11.5. One of its key differentiators, its ability to tie in both search engine optimization and Google AdWords, results in a single dashboard. Its search engine optimization features are the most robust of all of the tools reviewed, which makes sense because it started out as a search engine optimization research, benchmarking, and competitive analysis tool. Don't let that fool you; Raven doesn't shortchange the social channel in its analysis, but it has used the framework it created for SEO analysis to create a powerful platform that is affordable for companies of all sizes and allows for true cross-channel reporting.

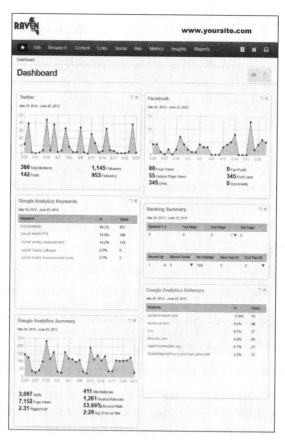

Figure 11.5 *Raven's mashup provides cross-channel reporting.*

Raven's monitoring features allow for keyword scans across social channels and web properties like blogs, forums, and answers sites. Its engagement features allow marketers to publish content, schedule content, assign tasks, and even add contacts with a mini-social CRM that allows tasks and notes to be assigned based on an individual. Marketers also can provide their blog login credentials and manage blog content right within the interface, and Raven provides an SEO analysis of the post. Raven's SEO suite allows marketers to do keyword research, which provides a mashup of data from SEMRush, SEOmoz, Google AdWords, and OpenCalais' Alchemy API. Marketers can also benchmark keywords, do competitive benchmarking, manage links, and produce reports on the results. This is just a small sampling of the SEO features available. Raven also pulls in data from Google AdWords to monitor and measure ad performance. When you're looking at the digital channel as a whole, Raven truly provides cross-channel capabilities that let marketers measure their results in one-easy-to-use interface. You can also link your MailChimp account to tie in email metrics. Raven's measurement capabilities are built upon a combination of third-party tools and its own data to provide a strong set of metrics that provide an almost one-stop shop for reporting.

Overall Measurement Features (3.3 Stars)

Raven allows marketers to create website profiles that are linked to a website address that is the end destination for traffic. Each of these profiles allows the marketer to add profiles for Twitter, Facebook, YouTube, Google AdWords, Google Analytics, MailChimp, and SEO rankings tied to the website profile. The overall dashboard is module based, which allows marketers to customize their view of data from all sources. Marketers can quickly segment and group data by creating different reporting profiles. The beauty of using third-party integrations as the basis of their analysis is that users can get historical data from applications that have been running for longer than the Raven Tools profile. This is limited to Facebook Insights, YouTube Insights, Google AdWords, Google Analytics, and MailChimp. Custom searches, SEO analysis, and Twitter begin collection at the date of account setup. Raven is a great tool for the marketer who is just starting to measure social media but will need some work to provide the in-depth analysis recommended in this book.

Third-Party Integrations (3.5 Stars)

The Raven system is built upon combining data from a variety of sources; therefore, it is the most advanced in terms of leveraging third-party APIs to provide cross-channel data. It provides a reasonable mashup of data, but it could pull in far more to provide marketers with deep dive capabilities. To reach a broader audience, Raven should look at integrating with more enterprise-level tools like

ExactTarget's Email System, for example. However, for most marketers, Raven provides a broad set of data. Raven should look to bring in more of the data that is available within the APIs of these tools. Currently, most of the data that is pulled in is available on front-page summary reports from the third-party tool and lacks depth that sophisticated marketers will want.

Social Media Data Tracking (3 Stars)

Marketers can get all the basic social media data out of Raven, including some metrics that aren't available easily, such as Twitter reach metrics. Most of this top-line data is available in other places, but what's unique here is that you have one interface and you can compare it to other digital marketing channels. Twitter data is focused on reach, engagement, connections, and site traffic with a referring URL from Twitter. This provides a nice overview of channel growth that displays in a graph. Facebook data pulls in most of the data available from Facebook Insights and adds in referral website traffic. YouTube Insights and MailChimp pretty much collect the same overview type of metrics. Where Raven really sets itself apart is with its ranking data. Users can input a set of keywords and easily pull in a dash-board to show changes in where their website is ranking for those keywords on Google, Yahoo, and Bing. Users can also provide a set of competitive websites and rank themselves against the competition. However, no in-depth data is being pro-vided here. It is straight summary and overview data that can be collected within most tools.

Conversion Tracking (3.5 Stars)

Raven pulls in conversion tracking from Google Analytics so marketers can see which of their social campaigns and social channels contributed. Raven also pulls in the source, medium, and campaign from custom URL parameters on shortened links within the Other Sources tab. In addition, it allows custom URL parameters to be added to every shortened URL, so campaign data will pass through and be shown with conversion reports. The only limitation is that you only get data that is shown in Google Analytics because Raven focuses on data aggregation instead of data creation.

Reporting Features (2.5 Stars)

Raven allows marketers to build reports using a modularized report creation wiz-ard. You select the modules you want and use the drag-and-drop interface to drag modules to the order you want. You can also create report templates so that you can produce multiple reports using the same modules and brand report templates that allow you to add your company's branding and allow agencies to white-label all their client reporting.

Report templates can be scheduled to go out by email at the desired frequency, and to a specified distribution list. The report can be delivered as a PDF or an Excel file. This automated reporting saves time when other stakeholders in the organization want insight into how digital channels are performing.

The only limitation is that marketers have little control over which metrics are shown in the report. All the metrics that are available in a module appear on the report. The only customization available is for the level of detail available within the module, such as daily, weekly, or monthly data. This means the reports are appropriate for manager-level reporting, but they quickly get too long for high-level executive reports.

Conversion Reporting (2.5 Stars)

Raven provides basic reporting for conversions through the Google Analytics interface. Marketers can see the referring channel and any custom URL parameters that were provided. However, these reports are fairly limited in the Google Analytics portion of the interface, and marketers can overlay other types of social data that would be interesting to compare.

Summary Report Features (2 Stars)

Raven allows for detailed overview reporting, but it fails to aggregate data from multiple channels into a quick summary report. Marketers can add a written summary that can be included in reports, but this is cumbersome and takes a lot of time for individual report analysis without having the data already organized into a summary.

Report Export and Customization (3 Stars)

Raven provides the best layout customization and export options for report generation of any of the tools reviewed. However, layering on more capability to customize the data represented would go a long way toward making the reporting more robust. Marketers cannot customize the metrics that are collected and provided in reports, nor can you customize the dashboard to highlight the key performance indicators for the organization. For example, there is a reporting module for Twitter that includes changes in followers, posts, retweets, replies and other mentions. Once the Twitter module is added to a report, all of those data points are included in the report. Some marketers will want more control over which data points are shown in reports so they can create high-level versus in-depth reports. This and the lack of depth in the data collected are Raven's biggest weaknesses.

Data Presentation (4 Stars)

Raven does provide an easily built, automated report that presents nicely, provided you don't include the modules that produce pages and pages of text data. Although the reports are nice and have helpful graphs of the data presented, the lack of user control over what is presented and the inability to provide user input into additional calculations needed for presentation makes it difficult to give Raven anything over 4 stars. It is providing a mashup of data that makes it easier for marketers to plug data points into a customized dashboard for presentation. However, its reports are unlikely to be the only ones provided to decision makers and frankly include too much data for an executive report.

Social Snap

Cost—Starts at $500 per month; custom report development and assistance with Google Analytics goals and funnel setup starts at $1,500

Classification—Measurement

Overall Rating—4.3 stars

Website—http://www.socialsnap.com

"Social Snap is the only social media measurement tool that integrates social media monitoring, web analytics data, and hundreds of social channel metrics into a single, easy-to-use interface. This powerful mashup of social media intelligence gives you the insights you need to optimize PR and marketing performance, maximize time and resources, and tie social media to business impact."

Overview

Social Snap is one of the few pure social media measurement tools out there (see Figure 11.6). Its team would be the first to tell you that it isn't trying to be a monitoring and engagement tool. Its goal is to provide the most comprehensive data set on social performance. This means it has a vast list of metrics available within the tool, and if a social channel doesn't provide it, it may have found somewhere else to get it. Social Snap doesn't just focus on detail-level data; it provides a nice balance between summary data and a detailed analytics review, which is great for the busy marketer who wants to get data at a glance and then drill down into the details.

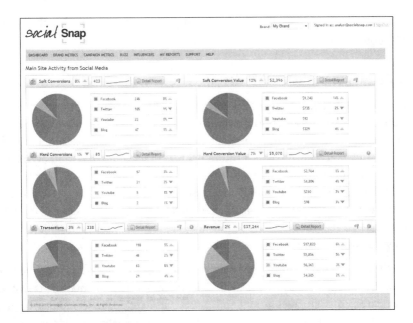

Figure 11.6   *Social Snap gets social media return on investment (ROI).*

(One nice thing is that Social Snap's reporting terminology is similar to the terminology throughout this book. Not much "translation" necessary.)

Social Snap provides an influencer section that tracks social conversations with influencers. However, it requires the user to manually put in the information related to his social profiles. It would be nice if this were automatically linked. Social Snap doesn't have the level of contact management that is available in Raven, and neither provides in-depth influencer outreach research. The influencer section is immature compared to true influencer management tools; it would be nice if Social Snap pulled data from more robust tools for marketers who are focused on influencer outreach.

Overall Measurement Features (4.3 Stars)

Any tool that provides more than 500 metrics from the social channel understands that data is king when it comes to showing social media ROI. Social Snap is focused on providing cross-channel and apples-to-apples comparisons across multiple digital marketing networks, including social channels and website activity. Social Snap's user interface has a grid-based system, and it provides nice little graphics along the way to provide an indication of growth or decline. It could certainly use a facelift to make the system easier to use and the data easier to understand once you start diving into the details. When you are looking at this level of detail, it is nice to have a balance between the nitty-gritty, line-level analysis and a quick graphic overview.

Third-Party Integrations (3.5 Stars)

Social Snap didn't build a social measurement tool from scratch because there is a plethora of data already spread out across the social web. Instead, Social Snap focused on a series of mashup data that is available within its interface, although it brings in a much fuller data set (more than 500+ social metrics) and even layers on derived metrics such as true Twitter network size and retweets per thousand followers. Its tool is designed for the sophisticated marketer to track social media down to onsite conversions. This is all facilitated through Google Analytics, which may be an issue for larger brands that are prevented from installing Google Analytics on their websites.

Social Snap chose to focus on the social channel, but it would be nice if it tied in multiple marketing channels like SEO, Google AdWords, and email. This would provide true cross-channel insight and, with its in-depth data, would be extremely powerful. Marketers typically manage more than just social media and are held accountable to cross-channel impact, so it would be nice to have all that data in one place.

Social Snap would also benefit from better monitoring functions, or integration that would allow it. Although its goal isn't to be a monitoring tool, it misses out on important monitoring metrics because it isn't collecting a robust enough data set. It monitors the social web, but in order to collect data from third party websites, the SocialSnap team must create a custom list of websites that will be scanned and included for each client. This is a bit of a cumbersome process when many true monitoring tools automatically scan millions of websites. This information would be helpful for marketers who want holistic reporting on the entire digital marketing channel. Monitoring tool integrations weren't available at the time of review, but Social Snap does allow marketers to import reports from its monitoring tool for inclusion in buzz reporting. It would also benefit from pulling in data from an influencer outreach tool that is focused on true influencer management and reporting, if it wants to have a robust influencer section as part of its tool.

Social Media Data Tracking (5 Stars)

If social media data exists, Social Snap is reporting on it. It offers the most comprehensive set of social media metrics available of the tools reviewed here. It boasts more than 500 social media metrics, either straight from social or web channels or derived from calculations it feels are important for social media marketers. Its influencer section also reports on a proprietary relevance score that it claims is more accurate than Klout.

Conversion Tracking (4.5 Stars)

Social Snap is smart about conversion tracking. It realizes that the ultimate conversion point tends to be on the company's website. Rather than building a proprietary conversion tracking mechanism, it focuses on pulling data from goals and funnels in Google Analytics. It will even help companies set up the proper goals and funnels within their Google Analytics account to ensure that conversions are tracked appropriately. However, it expects marketers to understand how to add Google Analytics custom URL parameters within its existing engagement tool. If not, it is dependent on the referring URL, which isn't always a social channel if there is an assisted social conversion. Social Snap will add in the social media assist and custom URL parameters as tracked through Google Analytics when it becomes available within the application programming interface (API), but this still won't provide the detailed, campaign-level detail marketers need to associate conversions with the content that is generating them.

Marketers want to know more than the social media channel that is generating a conversion; they want the exact status update that contributed or directly led to a conversion. But you have to give Social Snap props for pulling in Google Analytics conversion data, because it is the only one that was doing it at the time of the review. If you are using Google Analytics custom URL parameters on your shortened URLs (this will be explained in Chapter 12, "A Great Starter Mix of Tools for Less Than $10 a Month"), you will be able to get post-level analysis and conversion analysis within Social Snap's interface, or if Google ever opens the API. You can supplement Social Snap's conversion tracking with campaign-level reporting pulled from your campaign report from Google Analytics.

The biggest limitation here is that marketers have to be using Google Analytics and have goals and funnels set up to get conversion data. For most, this will make life easier. However, for some Fortune 500 brands, this may be a deal killer because many aren't allowed to install Google Analytics on their websites. Social Snap should include more web analytics tools to be a viable tool for more marketers.

Reporting Features (3.9 Stars)

With the level of metrics available in Social Snap, you would expect to be able to report on pretty much anything you want. And you can, provided it can be built within the available dashboards. Users can create customized report views and save them for quick analysis down the road. Reports can be created by channel or even for quick cross-channel analysis on predefined key performance indicators.

Conversion Reporting (4.75 Stars)

Social Snap outperforms other tools in terms of conversion reporting, provided the user has Google Analytics. It breaks down conversions into two key categories: soft conversions and hard conversions. Marketers can identify each of the goal conversions available in their Google Analytics account as either soft or hard, which will aggregate the conversions into the right bucket. This is broken down by social media channel: Twitter, Facebook, YouTube, and other social conversions. The only limitation is that Social Snap can't show campaign data associated with a conversion because it isn't available in the Google Analytics API. However, it is committed to adding it as soon as it is available.

Summary Report Features (5 Stars)

Social Snap understands that marketers and executives think different key performance indicators are important, so it has a "Favorite KPIs Dashboard" that is customizable for each user based upon any collected metric. Widgets on the home screen provide a quick glance of changes in reach and engagement on each social channel, and overall exposure, engagement, website conversions, and product recommendations at a glance.

Report Export and Customization (2 Stars)

Although users can customize the "Favorite KPIs Dashboard," they can't report or automatically schedule reports to be emailed. However, Social Snap has this feature on the development road map.

Data Presentation (5 Stars)

Social Snap aggregates a substantial amount of social data into its platform. Although it allows marketers to use monetary conversion values, it also aggregates actual revenue associated with onsite conversions tracked through Google Analytics. For marketers who do not sell products or services online, Social Snap also allows you to track campaign and marketing costs associated with the social media channel and provide cost-based reporting such as cost per conversion and cost per site visit. This is by far the best alignment to the recommendations in this book and the best way to present data and align social media to bottom-line results. The data points are aligned accurately, but the user interface and actual reports still need a designer's touch.

Tracx

> **Cost**—Starts at $3,000 per month for brands; agency licenses start at $2,200 per client
>
> **Classification**—Monitoring, Engagement, and Measurement
>
> **Overall Rating**—2.5 stars
>
> **Website**—http://www.tracx.com
>
> "Tracx is a NYC-based company with a SaaS platform for sophisticated brand marketers who want to do more than monitor their social media presence, but actually manage it. The company provides an end-to-end solution that indexes the entire social web and delivers the most relevant, high impact audiences and conversations by capturing a 360-degree view of activity around a brand. The platform allows marketers to sift through streams of social media data and drill down to provide geographic, demographic, and psychographic insights and to monitor performance against competitors while planning, monitoring, engaging, and measuring influencers all in one place."

Overview

Tracx positions itself as a monitoring, engagement, and measurement platform. It has the cleanest interface and aggregated reporting dashboard of all the tools reviewed, as shown in Figure 11.7. Its system provides full-scale monitoring of keyword mentions across Flickr, YouTube, Facebook, Twitter, forums, news sites, Tumblr, Instagram, 21 million blogs, LinkedIn, and retail sites like Amazon, Foursquare, Yelp, Yahoo Places, Reddit, and Get Glue. Posts can easily be assigned to other users and replied to within their interface. Tracx also has a feature designed to help with influencer outreach and fan engagement. One of the challenges with many tools is the ability to recognize that a fan on Facebook, a follower on Twitter, and a blogger are the same person. Yet Tracx has developed a proprietary algorithm that connects these profiles. In the example provided, Tracx mentioned that if a fan has a blog, and he promotes all his social profiles on his blog, the system will connect all these accounts with the individual user and display all his social profiles on his record.

As Tracx collects a lot of data through its monitoring tool, it also presents large amounts of data in a clean interface. Various reports are available, but one of the best ones places this data into a funnel graphic and shows user movement through the funnel. Although Tracx has the best user interface, it has some work to do on collecting and tracking the right pieces of data to enable full-scale reporting that would align with the recommendations throughout this book.

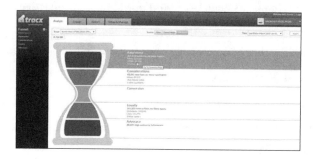

Figure 11.7   *Tracx displays data in a funnel, but it really looks like an hourglass.*

Overall Measurement Features (2.2 Stars)

Tracx aggregates all the data it collects into a simple, easy-to-read dashboard, despite the volume of data that is used to generate the reports. Although it has the standard monitoring and engagement metrics, it needs to boost its campaign management and conversion reporting to compete. It has the capability to do conversion reporting, but it requires the account team to customize and set it up for each client, which will be a challenge for marketers who have various campaigns that change over time, especially if it involves creating and deploying new conversion pages.

Third-Party Integrations (1.5 Stars)

Other than pulling data from Facebook Insights, Tracx doesn't have disclosed integrations with third-party data sources. It definitely doesn't integrate with web analytics packages. Tracx is limited to general social media data and doesn't pull in data from web analysis tools. Tracx can't compete with the other tools here.

Social Media Data Tracking (3.5 Stars)

In terms of social media data tracking, Tracx performs well. Although it doesn't pull in the level of data that Social Snap does, Tracx does an excellent job of displaying basic metrics that have large data sets behind them. Its interface uses a clean dashboard style with green and red arrows and even a "fuel gauge" type meter to show progress. This base level reporting is nice, but it isn't going to deliver proof of ROI.

Conversion Tracking (1.5 Stars)

It's hard to speak to the conversion tracking for Tracx because it wasn't able to produce an example of the tracking even though there is a clear space for it in Figure 11.7. Apparently, it requires custom setup for each client, which makes it cumbersome and difficult to implement. Tracx may charge more for the setup of conversion tracking, depending on the complexity of the project. It receives 1.5 stars because the capability is there, but the process is too cumbersome for most marketers. There weren't features shown for robust campaign management that would tie into reporting, either.

Reporting Features (3.1 Stars)

One nice thing about the data that is available through Tracx is that it allows you to slice and dice reporting using any of the data filters, brands, or keywords you have set up. This allows for quick comparisons across brands, competitors, or keywords.

Conversion Reporting (1.5 Stars)

Other than the funnel report showed in Figure 11.7, conversions weren't on any of the other reports. Tracx also didn't report on any other bottom-line metrics like cost, which could be an easy adjustment for it to align itself to business objectives. In this instance, conversions were reported at the highest overview level, without insight into any of the actual posts that led to a conversion.

Summary Report Features (4.2 Stars)

At the summary level, Tracx provides great overview information for a manager, minus the conversion piece. Its interface is super slick, and the imagery is compelling. It provides the summary chart on the top half of the interface and all the details on the bottom half. This allows a marketer to look for outliers and drill down into the post-level information.

Report Export and Customization (3.5 Stars)

Tracx has predefined and user-generated reports that can be saved and rerun at various intervals. You can export them as Excel, CSV, or PDF files.

Data Presentation (2 Stars)

The way Tracx presents data is beautiful, but the data points lack substance that would align with the other recommendations in the book. It may provide a great monitoring and engagement tool, but as a measurement tool it provides the same data that any tool will provide. For $3,000 a month, you wouldn't be selecting Tracx for its measurement capabilities; you'd select it for its monitoring and engagement features.

Summary

More than 20 tools were reviewed to select the most important to include in this chapter. Of all the tools available at that time, Social Snap's reporting methodologies aligned most closely with those presented in this book. The question becomes, "Do I have money for another social media tool?" For some companies, budget is hard to come by, so marketers need to show executives the ROI first. If that is the case, Chapter 12 will show you how to get pretty darned close to core business metrics using tools that cost less than $10 a month. They won't give you the detailed reporting that many of the tools here provide, but they'll allow you to tie social media links to web analytics and integrate campaign tracking, which is the glue that holds it all together.

Hands-On Exercise: Measurement Tool Worksheet

If you are reviewing your own social media monitoring system or are in the process of looking at other tools to fulfill your measurement needs, this checklist will help you compare apples to apples across multiple tools. This is a basic analysis organized by category. Each tool should receive 1 to 5 stars for each category. Only fill out the sections that relate to the reason you need the tool. For example, if you aren't looking for a monitoring and engagement tool, focus on the measurement section. If the tool you're reviewing also includes monitoring and engagement features, review them as compared to your current tool.

Use this chart to compare social media tools. Place a check box next to each area to show if the feature exists for the tools you are reviewing in the following categories.				
Place the name of the tool here -------------------->				
Monitoring Features				
Social Channel Searches				
Blog/Forum/Web Searches				
Engagement Features				
Publishing				
Scheduling				

Use this chart to compare social media tools. Place a check box next to each area to show if the feature exists for the tools you are reviewing in the following categories.				
Workflow Features				
Assign Posts				
Set Tasks				
See Completed Tasks				
Contact Management				
Measurement Features				
Third-Party Integrations				
Social Media Data Tracking				
Conversion Tracking				
Revenue Tracking				
Social Media Budget Tracking				
Reporting Features				
Conversion Reporting				
Summary Report Features				
Report Export and Customization				
Manager Data Presentation				
Executive Data Presentation				
Setup Price				
Monthly Price				
Other Fees				

12

A Great Starter Mix of Tools for Less Than $10 a Month

In the spirit of progress before perfection, the goal of this book is to give you a solution you can immediately implement while you build some of the more complicated pieces you'll need for full end-to-end measurement (or get budget approval for a more expensive tool). There's a solution available right now that will get you better data and tie the social channel into conversions. And it costs less than $10 a month. Sound too good to be true? It's not. That killer combination is HootSuite Pro and Google Analytics. This chapter shows you how these tools combine to give you better data than you've ever had and how to use them to produce reports that will make your executives sing your praises.

Many marketers are looking for a shiny new social media measurement tool without evaluating their current tools to see how they can get the data they need. This is unfortunate because most websites already have Google Analytics installed. And if they don't, it's a simple installation. Further, many organizations have integrated Google Analytics campaign data into their customer relationship management (CRM) because there has been so much investment into other types of marketing that are tracked using the system. To see if you have an integration in place, look at the lead sources that are in your CRM system. If you see clients with lead sources of Organic, PPC, or specific web-based campaign names, it's highly likely you already have this integration. While you're on your quest for that shiny software box, you can start taking advantage of the tools you already have to show the data you want.

Why HootSuite Pro Is a Crucial Part of the Mix

HootSuite Pro's best-kept secret is that it can be integrated with Google Analytics to provide campaign-based tracking on every uniform resource locator (URL) that's shortened and shared on a social channel. If you're already using Google Analytics, you won't have to add any special code to your site. That means you don't have to wait for your IT team to do anything—you can immediately start getting higher-value information about how the social channel is delivering. To use the features described in the rest of this chapter, you need a HootSuite Pro account, which costs $9.99 a month for the first user.

Validating Google Analytics Setup

The first step is to validate that your Google Analytics account has been properly set up. Simply having the Google Analytics code on your site isn't enough. You need to have goals and funnels defined. Goals and funnels allow you to tell Google Analytics where your conversion points are on the site. With this feature, you can track how many website visitors convert, where they convert, and what referring URL or campaign drove the conversion. Google Analytics allows you to define up to ten pages that lead to a goal conversion. These are called *funnels*, and they allow you to track through an entire conversion process and help you identify where people fall off so you can work to optimize the process later. You can find step-by-step instructions for setting up goals and funnels by searching for "How do I set up goals and funnels?" within the Google Analytics Help Center.

Setting up goals and funnels requires some thinking up front. It's best to work backward from the end of your conversion process, so think about what kind of thank-you and confirmation pages you have on your site—subscription confirmation pages, registration confirmation pages, and product purchase confirmation pages are all conversion points. The conversion point is on the thank-you or confirmation page because the only way a visitor can get to those pages is by going through the entire process. If you put the conversion point on the page that promotes your newsletter sign-up, for example, you would have data with false conversions because more people may view that page than actually go through the process to sign up. Create a list of all of your thank-you and confirmation pages.

Then create a list of all the pages that are included in the process to get to each thank-you or confirmation page. This can include the page to promote the conversion point, such as the page that promotes a newsletter sign-up. Worksheets to accomplish this are provided in the hands-on exercise at the end of this chapter. When you are finished, you should have a good understanding of the entire conversion process for each of your conversion points. This entire process will allow you to set up a "funnel" within Google Analytics that tracks each step in the process through the resulting conversion.

This is important because you want to understand where people "fall off" or exit the process. These exit pages will be good opportunities for optimization to attempt to increase throughput and higher conversion rates. Don't go too crazy here; if a page isn't part of the actual conversion process, don't include it. The goal isn't to track every entry point in the site that leads to a conversion; it is to track the conversion process. Entry points to the site can be reviewed with a path analysis later and do not require additional setup. Once you have your conversion process defined, the next step is to make sure it is set up correctly in Google Analytics.

To do this, log in to Google Analytics and go to the admin panel; then click Goals. You should have a screen that is similar to the one shown in Figure 12.1. This screen shows you the goals that have already been set up in Google Analytics. Hopefully, you will see that your goals have already been set up for the conversion points you've defined. If you don't, define the goals you need added with the process for conversion and either work with your IT team to set them up or set them up yourself. You can find instructions by searching for "setting up goals" in the Google Analytics help center. If you have a complex site with multiple conversion points and funnels already established, work with your IT team before you adjust anything. You could break something important.

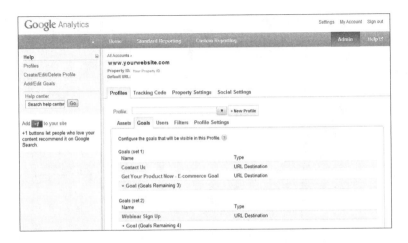

Figure 12.1 *Goals are shown in the Google Analytics admin panel.*

To validate that the goals have been set up correctly and they align with the conversion process you defined, click on one of the goals in the admin panel. You should see a screen that looks like Figure 12.2. As shown in the Goal Funnel section, multiple pages are involved in the webinar registration process, including the webinar landing page, registration page, and thank-you page. Each of these has been defined, so it's easy to tell where people fall off in the process. For example, if people from the landing page click to register, and a high percentage of visitors don't complete the process, it may be a sign that the registration process is too complex or requests more information than participants are willing to share. This can be modified and tested to see if you can increase the percentage of people who complete the registration. You learned earlier that social media leads are different from other leads because they tend to be earlier in the buying cycle. If your forms are driving social media leads away, it may be time to reevaluate. But you won't know unless you're tracking through the funnel. You also want to make sure the pages listed in these goal funnels are actually part of the process to convert. It's common to find goals that haven't been set up properly, so check them closely.

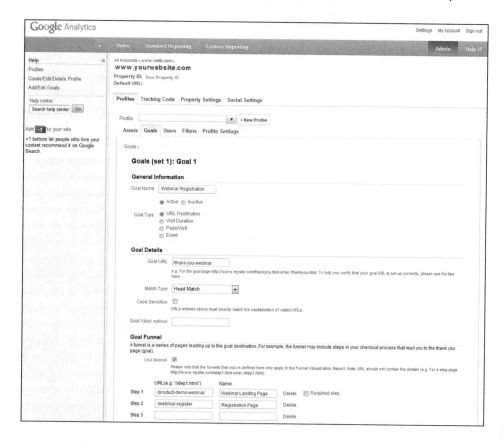

Figure 12.2 *Clicking a goal reveals the goal funnel that has been established.*

There's one field in Figure 12.2 that's worth spending some time discussing—the optional Goal Value field. Placing a value in this field attaches a monetary value for each goal conversion. If you're putting values in this field for conversions that don't generate revenue, stop! In the example of the webinar sign-up sample in Figure 12.2, there isn't a value in the field. That's because someone attending a free webinar doesn't generate revenue. Revenue is generated when that person becomes a client. If you place a value in that field, and it doesn't actually generate revenue, you're presenting fluff data that doesn't correlate to real revenue. Working with fluff data can lead to bad decisions that hurt real revenue.

That's a sure-fire way to get a skeptical executive to question the credibility of your data. If other marketing channels in your organization attach a monetary value to these types of conversions, you may have to do the same to be sure you can compare apples to apples. But it may be time to sit down with the executive team and make the case that the practice should be stopped. You'll gain credibility with the executive team for questioning and pulling the rug out from under this falsely represented data.

Integrating HootSuite with Google Analytics

Now that you have Google Analytics set up and ready to track your social data, get HootSuite set up to do the same. If you have a HootSuite Pro account, there's a feature that opens the golden egg to awesome data, but you have to know it exists to find it. But first, integrate your Google Analytics account with HootSuite.

1. Log into HootSuite.

2. Hover over the navigation bar to the right.

3. Click Analytics (see Figure 12.3).

4. Click Quick Analytics.

5. Click Google Analytics.

6. Click Add Google Profile.

You'll be asked to authenticate your Google Analytics account to complete the setup. That's it.

Figure 12.3   *Hover over HootSuite's right navigation bar to reveal the Analytics option.*

Start Tracking

Now you're ready to start adding campaign data to your shortened URLs. This process is simple; once you get it down, it will become second nature. The goal is to add Google Analytics custom URL parameters to any URL shared on a social network that drives users back to one of your company's website properties. Although HootSuite will allow you to add the parameters to any link, adding it to third-party URLs just pushes data into their Google Analytics account, rather than your own.

1. Go to the HootSuite dashboard and click in the Compose Message field.

2. Type a status update as you normally would and add a link to the Link field. But don't shorten it just yet. This is where you'll find HootSuite's golden egg.

3. Click the little grayed-out gear to the right of the link you just added. *Note: The gear only appears if your cursor is in the Link field.* Are you ready to have your social media data analysis changed forever? When you click on the gear, you should see a screen like Figure 12.4.

Note

The gear only appears if your cursor is in the Link field.

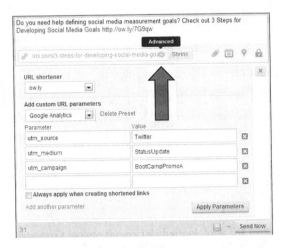

Figure 12.4 *Click the grayed-out gear next to your link to reveal the Advanced panel.*

4. Click the drop-down under Add Custom URL Parameters and select Google Analytics.

5. Type your campaign source, medium, and campaign in the fields provided, click Apply Parameters, and then click Shrink.

You can check that the campaign parameters were added before you shrink by placing your cursor in the Link field and pressing the right arrow to scroll through the link. You should see something resembling http://socialmediaexplorer.com/?utm_source=NicholeKelly&utm_medium=IsAwesome&utm_campaign=SingItWithMe. If you have extra time on your hands, you can add campaign parameters like the ones in the example on links for third-party websites. In the example, Google Analytics would show NicholeKelly as the source, IsAwesome as the medium, and SingItWithMe as the campaign for the traffic and conversions that were driven on the third-party site. It's at least good for a chuckle.

This process appended the values you put in the Campaign, Medium, and Source fields to the end of the URL using the necessary format for Google Analytics to capture them. The way you use these fields requires some planning to get the most effective data when you pull reports later. You have three fields to add anything you want to show up in your Google Analytics reports, but you should use them with a purpose. Here are examples of ways you can use the fields.

Sample A

Source—Social Media Channel Content Is Posted On, such as Twitter

Medium—Type of Content Posted, such as Blog Post

Campaign—Content Title or Campaign Name, such as 5_Ways_to_Measure_Social_Media1

This is useful for companies that have one corporate social media account for each channel but want to understand the types of content that are driving the most traffic.

Sample B

Source—Social Media Channel Content Is Posted On, such as Twitter

Medium—Social Media Account Posting the Content, such as Nichole_Kelly

Campaign—Content Type and Shortened Title, such as Blog_SM_Measure_2

This is useful for companies that manage multiple social media accounts and want to be able to tell which accounts drive the most traffic and conversions.

Sample C

Source—Social Media Channel Content Is Posted On, such as Twitter

Medium—Content Type and Title, such as Blog_SM_Measure_3

Campaign—Campaign Name, such as Minneapolis_Event_Promo1

This is useful for tracking a specific promotional campaign while still capturing the content type and title.

Whatever system you choose, make sure everyone managing your social media channels uses that same system. This will produce meaningful data that you can compare and that has a clear connection to the content you're posting.

Tip

Keep all the status updates posted in an Excel file and number them. Then place an extra number at the end of the title or promotional campaign name that correlates to the status update posted. When you pull your reports, you'll be able to tell exactly which status updates generated the highest conversions.

Limitations

There are a couple of limitations. First, for HootSuite, if you want to post the same status update to Twitter and Facebook at the same time, you'll apply the same parameters to the URL, and you won't be able to tell whether resulting traffic and conversations came from Facebook or Twitter. There's a work-around that only adds a second to your posting process: Create the status update the first time, place Twitter in the Source field, and post. Copy the status update (without the link so it doesn't add the old parameters), add the original link, change the Source field to Facebook, and post. It takes only a second or two and makes all the difference when you pull your data. Although Google Analytics has attempted to track all social media data for you within the social reports dashboard, this provides a second check because there have been drastic variations reported between known traffic that has been tagged with campaign parameters and what shows up in social reports.

Second, if you don't track e-commerce within Google Analytics, you won't be able to tie your results to revenue without an integration into your CRM. For some, a CRM integration may already be in place, or they track sales through Google Analytics already and this solution closes the gap between social media and other marketing channels. For others, it will provide the baseline data to start building toward full ROI analysis.

Getting the Data

Test to make sure your data is tracking correctly. To find it, log in to Google Analytics. Google changes the interface every once in a while, but look for the Traffic Sources page. Once there, drill down to campaign data (see Figure 12.5).

There are a few options for how you can view this data. For a quick glance, you can click on Source/Medium. Behind the graph, you will see tabs for each of your goals. Click one of your goals. When you do this, you can see each campaign source and medium with the goal conversion rate for each line.

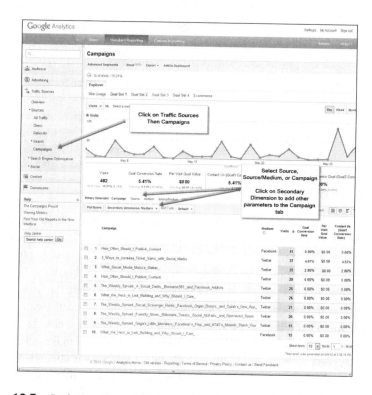

Figure 12.5 *Find your campaign data in Google Analytics.*

Notice that the data is perfect for managers. There are granular details like which content drove the most conversions. This is important so that you understand what is and what isn't working. Now you can optimize your content so that you can increase your conversion rates.

Google Analytics has also done some work to help you solve the problem of reporting on social media assists. There's a section under Traffic Sources called Social. Click this, and you'll see several reports available on the social channel. The most interesting report is found in the Overview report (see Figure 12.6), which shows where social fits into overall site traffic and conversions. An *assisted social conversion* is one that converted under a nonsocial campaign but at some point came to the site through a social campaign. The *last interaction social conversions* are ones that came from the social channel and converted. Social media was the last touch before the conversion. This data can be extremely powerful for market-ers because it's the first step to solving the campaign history problem. However, the big challenge is that you can't audit this data. Google Analytics doesn't show which campaign-assisted social conversions actually converted under, so there's no insight into which types of campaigns social is assisting. Is social helping SEO, PPC, direct traffic, or something else? You won't know.

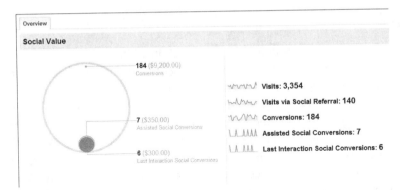

Figure 12.6   *Google Analytics Reports on the Social Media Assist*

Additionally, if you're using custom URL parameters on shortened URLs, you will know exactly how many site visits you drove to your own content from the social channel. The one gap will be the traffic that came from links shared from third parties. Social reports should capture all that traffic, so you would expect the social reports data to be higher than what shows in your campaign reports. Reporting for SME Digital clients has seen the opposite. Campaign reporting is showing up to three times more traffic than social reports, which doesn't make sense because all the traffic reported in campaigns that have a social media campaign assigned should show up in the social report dashboard as well. The lesson: You should proceed with cautious optimism when reviewing the social reports. It's a fairly new feature for Google Analytics, so it's likely to get better. But don't hang your reputation on the data until you can successfully audit and verify the data within the dashboard.

All this data is great, but simply spitting out a Google Analytics report isn't going to cut it with your executive team. The next chapter shows you how to use this data, or data you get from any of the measurement tools, to create a cross-channel dashboard with the data you need and the data your executive team wants.

Hands-On Exercise: Create a System for Using Custom URL Parameters

For the tips in this chapter to be effective, it will be important to have a repeatable and scalable system for how you will use the custom URL parameters in HootSuite. Even if you use a measurement tool other than Google Analytics, following these steps will allow you to have a secondary data source to validate your data. You'll be focused on three fields.

Source

The Source field typically designates where website traffic came from. This is a good place to put the social media channel where you posted the status update. Because you'll be typing in the Source field every time, it's crucial to have a consistent naming convention to ensure your reports are categorizing traffic correctly. If sometimes you use *Facebook* and other times you use *FB* or *FBook*, it will take more work to aggregate data for your reports. The beauty of having a consistent naming convention is that you'll be able to do searches within the campaign report to quickly aggregate data and get a summary of all the traffic and conversions that came from the social channel. If you don't, you'll have to try to remember all the combinations you used, search for them individually, and then document the summary data in Excel so you can aggregate the numbers and get a final summary report. That's a lot of unnecessary work.

Come up with a standard name for each social network that you'll use in the Source field. Use the following table to document all the social media networks you use to publish content that drives users back to your site. Once it's complete, provide the list of names to anyone who will be managing your social networks.

Social Media Channel	Name to Use in Source Field
Facebook	FB

Medium

You can use the Medium parameter in a variety of ways. The best way to use the field for your company depends on the complexity of your social media use. As an example, think about how HubSpot uses social media. It has several employees publishing content on its behalf. Each uses a personal social account to promote resources available on the HubSpot website. If HubSpot wants to understand which social media account drove the most traffic, it could use the medium to specify the social media account used to post the status update. This would let HubSpot aggregate all the data from its corporate and employee accounts and easily drill down to a specific user to see the traffic and conversions that account drove for the company.

For companies that use a single corporate account to promote content available on their site, using the social media account in the Medium field would be a waste of an opportunity to get other types of data. They may be interested in learning which type of content is driving the most traffic. Therefore, they could use the Medium field to track the content type, such as blog post, video, poll, e-book, webinar, or any other type of content they publish on their website. Again, it will be important to have a naming convention for how these content types are referenced in the Custom URL field.

Think about the best way your company could use the Medium field and use one of the following tables to document how you will use it to provide better data. Then provide this chart to anyone who is managing your social networks.

Social Media Account	Name to Use in the Medium Field
@ComcastBetty	Betty

Content Type	Name to Use in the Medium Field
E-Book	EBook

 Note

You can't use spaces or several types of characters in these fields. It's best to come up with combinations of letters to represent the medium. However, try to think of words that don't require a secret decoder ring to figure out.

Campaign

The Campaign field may be one of the most challenging to standardize because there are so many ways you can use it. Some companies have robust marketing campaigns that are run throughout the year. In that instance, use the campaign name in this field. Just make sure there's an agreed-upon naming convention for campaigns, and confirm what will be used as the medium as part of the process for campaign development.

For marketers who have campaign- and noncampaign-related content, this is a little more difficult. Sometimes they'll want to track the campaign, but for non-campaign-related content, they may want to track the name of the article or post they're promoting. There isn't a right answer here; what's important is that you use the field to track the information you want to show up in your reports.

For marketers who don't run extensive campaigns, the answer is far simpler. You can use the Campaign field to specify the name of the article or piece of content you're promoting. This lets you track conversions down to actual pieces of content. You can use the title of a blog post, the title of an e-book or webinar, or the title of any other type of content you're promoting. You may want to abbreviate the name, and you won't be able to use spaces. For example, if you were promoting a blog post titled "6 Ways to Track Social Media Campaigns," you could use a value such as 6WaysToTrackSMCampaigns.

Think about how you can use the Campaign field and define your approach to using the field. Use the following questionnaire to walk through the decisions you need to make.

Question	Yes	No
Will you use the name of the marketing campaign rather than the name of the content if the content is related to a campaign?		
Will you use the name of the content you're promoting when it isn't related to a specific campaign?		
Will you always use the name of the content regardless of the campaign it supports?		

Bonus Tip: Track the Exact Status Update That Drove a Conversion

To optimize your status updates, you can keep track of which version and type of status update drove a conversion by adding some additional information in the Campaign Parameter field. However, this requires a little extra work in HootSuite and Google Analytics.

To be effective, you need to keep a database of all the status updates you have posted on each social network. Create a unique identifier for each status update. An easy way to do this is to number them. Then label each status update with the type of status update it is, such as question, tip, photo, fact, or trivia. Then when you add your custom URL parameter for the medium, include the number and content type at the end. In the example that was used earlier, this would look like 6WaysToTrackSMCampaigns12Tip. When you look at the data in Google Analytics, you can cross-reference the number 12 to the post it corresponds to and see which status update drove the conversion. You can also do a search in Google Analytics for Tip to aggregate all the conversions with Tip in the campaign parameters to see how many conversions Tips created. Now you'll really have excellent data that can help you optimize your status updates and produce more of the updates that drive the most conversions.

## 13

Creating a Cross-Functional Measurement Dashboard

One of the most important elements in measuring social media is comparing social media within the context of how other marketing channels are performing. Although it's great to have an awesome social media measurement tool pumping out amazing data, it's not going to be enough to get the job done. You need to put together a reporting dashboard that collects both manager- and executive-level data and that is easy to update. You've spent time understanding what types of data you need to collect. Now it's time to organize them into a powerful presentation format that will make your bosses say, "Wow!"

This entire chapter is a hands-on exercise that will require a few things: you, your computer, and Microsoft Excel or an equivalent. Read through the whole chapter first to learn exactly what you need before you sit down to build your own dashboard. The first step is to define which marketing channels will be compared in your report, so you can show how social media is contributing to overall marketing success. Specifically, you should focus on marketing channels where your company puts significant focus and budget.

Social media can complement several marketing channels, sometimes effortlessly. These include, but are not limited to, PR, search engine optimization (SEO), online advertising, TV advertising, radio advertising, print advertising, email marketing, direct mail, and events. The easiest way to figure out which channels you should compare to is to get a copy of the executive marketing report, if you haven't already. This will show you what kind of data your executive team is looking for and which marketing channels have been defined as important contributors to the bottom line. If you can't get your hands on that report, create a list of all the marketing channels your company invests in and start there.

Your objective at the end of this chapter is to have two things built: an executive dashboard that is presentation-ready, and a marketing channel dashboard that provides all the detail you need to monitor your progress.

To get started, you need a complete list of metrics for the executive level and the manager level. The hands-on exercises from Chapters 4 and 8 will help. These are metrics that you determined were relevant to your company. Then breeze back over Chapter 6, "Measuring Social Media for Lead Generation," and look at the metrics listed for lead generation. At a minimum, use these metrics as a starting point. First, break them up into two categories: executive-level and manager-level metrics.

If you were able to get a copy of your executive marketing report, the executive-level metrics will be there. Each of these marketing channels typically has someone responsible for its marketing strategy. Ask that person for a sample of the reports he uses to monitor success on a monthly basis. This will give you the metrics you will collect for the manager-level dashboard. You can choose how detailed you want to get in your manager-level reporting for other marketing channels. You can keep it simple and look at one or two core metrics that drive the results you will see in the executive dashboard, or you can build out a full cross-functional dashboard that the entire marketing department can use. Whichever path you choose, remember progress before perfection. Start with something small, and move into something more robust after you have shown this type of reporting helps make better business decisions.

Now that you have a starting point, it's time to make Excel your best friend. Rest assured, the time you put in on the front end will build a powerful dashboard that will bring big dividends later. If you do it right the first time, the only thing you'll have to do later is update the report with the numbers for the reporting period. So roll up your sleeves and get this done.

To effectively build any Excel report, you need a plan for organizing the data. You're going to start by building a manager-level dashboard called the Marketing Channel Dashboard. The report will be broken into three core categories: exposure metrics, engagement metrics, and conversion metrics. Ultimately, all your data will tie into cost per impression, cost per engagement, and cost per conversion. You also will want to be able to compare month-over-month changes and understand the year-to-date results. Figure 13.1 shows an example of a starting point for the Marketing Channel Dashboard. You want to plug in the three categories of metrics and columns for each of the metrics you will consistently track in each category.

Exposure Metrics	Total Impressions	Prior Month	M/M %	YTD	Budget	Cost Per Impression
Engagement Metrics	Total Engagements	Prior Month	M/M%	YTD	Budget	Cost Per Engagement
Conversion Metrics	Total Conversions	Prior Month	M/M%	YTD	Budget	Cost Per Conversion

Figure 13.1 *Start by setting up your measurement categories and core metrics.*

Now for the fun part. You can do this in one of two ways. You can create a separate tab for exposure, engagement, and conversions to keep your report clean. Or you can build out the sections between these categories. If you choose to use a single worksheet for your report, it's best to put the data in each section in groups so you can quickly expand and collapse sections. Whichever path you choose, the next step is to input each of the marketing channels as a subcategory under each category. Then you'll add all the metrics you'll track for each one. Remember, you need to align these metrics to use the same language, so group them into items that can be termed Impressions, Engagements, and Conversions. If they don't fit into those three categories, throw them out; they're probably fluff.

Focus on exposure metrics first. Create a subcategory for each marketing channel, and then add in the metrics that can be measured as an impression. Remember: This represents the holistic audience of people who may have seen your brand based on the activities from each of the marketing channels. See Figure 13.2 for an example of what your dashboard could look like.

Exposure Metrics	Total Impressions	Prior Month	M/M %	YTD	Budget	Cost Per Impression
Public Relations						
PR Mention Impressions			#DIV/0!			#DIV/0!
Total	0		#DIV/0!		$ -	#DIV/0!
Advertising						
Search Impressions			#DIV/0!			#DIV/0!
Display Impressions			#DIV/0!			#DIV/0!
Facebook Ad Impressions			#DIV/0!			#DIV/0!
Traditional Advertising Impressions			#DIV/0!			#DIV/0!
Total	0		#DIV/0!		$ -	#DIV/0!
Events						
Total Attendees			#DIV/0!			#DIV/0!
Total	0		#DIV/0!		$ -	#DIV/0!
Social Media						
Facebook Total Reach			#DIV/0!			#DIV/0!
Twitter Reach			#DIV/0!			#DIV/0!
SocialToaster Twitter Reach			#DIV/0!			#DIV/0!
SocialToaster Facebook Reach			#DIV/0!			#DIV/0!
SocialToaster LinkedIn Reach			#DIV/0!			#DIV/0!
SocialToaster MySpace Reach			#DIV/0!			#DIV/0!
Total	0	0	#DIV/0!	0	$ -	#DIV/0!
Grand Total/Average	0	0			0	#DIV/0!

Figure 13.2 *Marketing Channel Dashboard Exposure section*

Now it's time to move into engagement metrics. This likely will be the biggest section in your report because there are so many forms of engagement with social media. Figure 13.3 shows a sample of what the Engagement section could look like. Think about what the different forms of engagement are for each marketing channel. PR has two primary forms of engagement: mentions and site visits that are generated from those mentions. Online advertising has two primary forms of engagement that wouldn't fall into the conversion category: a click and a site visit. Notice in Figure 13.3 that Facebook advertising is in the Advertising section rather than the Social Media section. It's important to separate paid versus earned media channels. Because Facebook ads are a form of paid advertising, it's best to include the results in the Advertising section so it can be compared to other forms of advertising and doesn't get mixed into earned social media results. Remember: The goal is to compare apples to apples. Facebook advertising's apple is online advertising.

Engagement Metrics	Total Engagements	Prior Month	M/M%	YTD	Budget	Cost Per Engagement
Public Relations						
PR Mentions			#DIV/0!		$ -	#DIV/0!
Site Visits from Media Mentions			#DIV/0!		$ -	#DIV/0!
Total	0		#DIV/0!		$ -	#DIV/0!
Advertising						
Search Clicks/ Site Visits			#DIV/0!		$ -	#DIV/0!
Display Clicks/ Site Visits			#DIV/0!		$ -	#DIV/0!
Facebook Clicks/ Site Visits			#DIV/0!		$ -	#DIV/0!
Traditional Advertising Clicks			#DIV/0!			#DIV/0!
Total	0		#DIV/0!		$ -	#DIV/0!
Events						
Total Contacts Made			#DIV/0!			
Total	0		#DIV/0!		$ -	#DIV/0!
Social Media						
Facebook Engagement						
Page Likes			#DIV/0!		$ -	#DIV/0!
Engaged Users			#DIV/0!		$ -	#DIV/0!
Talking about us			#DIV/0!		$ -	#DIV/0!
Clicks on Content			#DIV/0!		$ -	#DIV/0!
Site Visits			#DIV/0!		$ -	#DIV/0!
Total	0		#DIV/0!		$ -	#DIV/0!
Twitter Engagement						
Followers			#DIV/0!			#DIV/0!
Clicks on Content			#DIV/0!			#DIV/0!
Mentions			#DIV/0!			#DIV/0!
ReTweets			#DIV/0!			#DIV/0!
Direct Messages			#DIV/0!			#DIV/0!
Site Visits			#DIV/0!			#DIV/0!
Total	0		#DIV/0!		$ -	#DIV/0!
LinkedIn Engagement						#DIV/0!
Followers			#DIV/0!			#DIV/0!
Clicks on Content			#DIV/0!			
Links Shared			#DIV/0!			#DIV/0!
Unique Visitors			#DIV/0!			#DIV/0!
ReTweets			#DIV/0!			#DIV/0!
Direct Messages			#DIV/0!			#DIV/0!
Site Visits			#DIV/0!			#DIV/0!
Total	0		#DIV/0!		$ -	#DIV/0!
SocialToaster Engagement						#DIV/0!
Super Fans			#DIV/0!			#DIV/0!
Twitter Super Fans			#DIV/0!			#DIV/0!
Facebook Super Fans			#DIV/0!			#DIV/0!
LinkedIn Super Fans			#DIV/0!			#DIV/0!
MySpace Super Fans			#DIV/0!			#DIV/0!
Links Shared			#DIV/0!			#DIV/0!
Site Visits			#DIV/0!			#DIV/0!
Unique Visitors			#DIV/0!			#DIV/0!
ReTweets			#DIV/0!			#DIV/0!
Direct Messages			#DIV/0!			#DIV/0!
Total	0		#DIV/0!		$ -	#DIV/0!
Grand Total/Average	0				$ -	#DIV/0!

Figure 13.3 *Marketing Channel Dashboard Engagement section.*

The good news is that the rest is a cakewalk from here. Your next section is the Conversion section. Conversions are conversions. There isn't a list of varied metrics that are being rolled up and normalized to make them easy to understand like you've seen in the prior sections. You'll want to break down your Conversion section into three categories: soft conversions, hard conversions, and product sales. The dashboard used in Figures 13.1 through 13.5, as an example, is a cost-based view of the data. So you won't see revenue numbers. However, you'll want to have a supplement to the conversion section that measures revenue if you're able to accurately get revenue data tied to the social channel. Remember: This doesn't mean you put in a "conversion value" in Google Analytics and track it as revenue. This means you can actually associate a sale that came from someone who has touched the social channel or directly converted from the social channel. Figure 13.4 provides a sample of what your Conversion section could look like.

Conversion Metrics	Total Conversions	Prior Month	M/M%	YTD	Budget	Cost Per Conversion
Public Relations						
Soft Conversions						
Contact Us			#DIV/0!			#DIV/0!
Informational Webinar Sign Up			#DIV/0!			#DIV/0!
Informational E-Book Download			#DIV/0!			
Partner Inquiry			#DIV/0!			#DIV/0!
Hard Conversions						
Schedule a Demo			#DIV/0!			#DIV/0!
Product Webinar Sign Up			#DIV/0!			#DIV/0!
Decision Making E-Book Download			#DIV/0!			
Free Trial			#DIV/0!			#DIV/0!
Sales						
Product Sales			#DIV/0!			
Total	0		#DIV/0!	$ -		#DIV/0!
Advertising						
Soft Conversions						
Contact Us			#DIV/0!			#DIV/0!
Informational Webinar Sign Up			#DIV/0!			#DIV/0!
Informational E-Book Download			#DIV/0!			#DIV/0!
Partner Inquiry			#DIV/0!			#DIV/0!
Hard Conversions						
Schedule a Demo			#DIV/0!			#DIV/0!
Product Webinar Sign Up			#DIV/0!			#DIV/0!
Decision Making E-Book Download			#DIV/0!			#DIV/0!
Free Trial			#DIV/0!			#DIV/0!
Sales						
Product Sales			#DIV/0!			#DIV/0!
Total	0		#DIV/0!	$ -		#DIV/0!
Events						
Soft Conversions						
Contact Us			#DIV/0!			#DIV/0!
Informational Webinar Sign Up			#DIV/0!			#DIV/0!
Informational E-Book Download			#DIV/0!			#DIV/0!
Partner Inquiry			#DIV/0!			#DIV/0!
Hard Conversions						
Schedule a Demo			#DIV/0!			#DIV/0!
Product Webinar Sign Up			#DIV/0!			#DIV/0!
Decision Making E-Book Download			#DIV/0!			#DIV/0!
Free Trial			#DIV/0!			#DIV/0!
Sales						
Product Sales			#DIV/0!			#DIV/0!
Total				$ -		
Social Media						
Facebook Conversions						
Soft Conversions						
Contact Us			#DIV/0!			#DIV/0!
Informational Webinar Sign Up			#DIV/0!			#DIV/0!
Informational E-Book Download			#DIV/0!			#DIV/0!
Partner Inquiry			#DIV/0!			#DIV/0!
Hard Conversions						
Schedule a Demo			#DIV/0!			#DIV/0!
Product Webinar Sign Up			#DIV/0!			#DIV/0!
Decision Making E-Book Download			#DIV/0!			#DIV/0!
Free Trial			#DIV/0!			#DIV/0!
Sales						
Product Sales			#DIV/0!			#DIV/0!
Total				$ -		
Twitter Conversions						
Soft Conversions						
Contact Us			#DIV/0!			#DIV/0!
Informational Webinar Sign Up			#DIV/0!			#DIV/0!
Informational E-Book Download			#DIV/0!			#DIV/0!
Partner Inquiry			#DIV/0!			#DIV/0!
Hard Conversions						
Schedule a Demo			#DIV/0!			#DIV/0!
Product Webinar Sign Up			#DIV/0!			#DIV/0!
Decision Making E-Book Download			#DIV/0!			#DIV/0!
Free Trial			#DIV/0!			#DIV/0!
Sales						
Product Sales			#DIV/0!			#DIV/0!
Total				$ -		
Grand Total/Average						

Figure 13.4 *Marketing Channel Dashboard Conversion section*

Okay, the hard part is done. Seriously. The rest is just aggregating data into a summary report for your executive dashboard. Create a new tab and title it Executive Dashboard. Copy over the Exposure, Engagement and Conversion categories and the marketing channels you're tracking under each one. Then start plugging in the formulas to bring in the summary data you collected in your Marketing Channel Dashboard. It's important that you take the time to build out these formulas because it will save you tremendous time whenever you need to update the report. Figure 13.5 shows an example of an Executive Dashboard. You'll use the Executive Dashboard to summarize data from the marketing channel and present it in a way that executives can quickly scan and understand. You can add other types of metrics, like conversion rates and revenue, to your reports to make them even more powerful.

social media explorer		EXECUTIVE DASHBOARD					
Exposure Metrics	Total Impressions	Prior Month	M/M%	YTD	Budget		Cost Per Impression
Public Relations					$	-	#DIV/0!
Advertising					$	-	#DIV/0!
Events					$	-	#DIV/0!
Social Media					$	-	#DIV/0!
Total/Average	-				$	-	**#DIV/0!**
Engagement Metrics	Total Engagements	Prior Month	M/M%	YTD	Budget		Cost Per Engagement
Public Relations					$	-	#DIV/0!
Advertising					$	-	#DIV/0!
Events					$	-	#DIV/0!
Social Media					$	-	#DIV/0!
Total/Average	-				$	-	**#DIV/0!**
Conversion Metrics	Total Conversions	Prior Month	M/M%	YTD	Budget		Cost Per Conversion
Public Relations					$	-	#DIV/0!
Soft Conversions					$	-	#DIV/0!
Hard Conversions					$	-	#DIV/0!
Product Sales					$	-	#DIV/0!
Advertising					$	-	#DIV/0!
Soft Conversions					$	-	#DIV/0!
Hard Conversions					$	-	#DIV/0!
Product Sales					$	-	#DIV/0!
Events					$	-	#DIV/0!
Soft Conversions					$	-	#DIV/0!
Hard Conversions					$	-	#DIV/0!
Product Sales					$	-	#DIV/0!
Social Media					$	-	#DIV/0!
Soft Conversions					$	-	#DIV/0!
Hard Conversions					$	-	#DIV/0!
Product Sales					$	-	#DIV/0!
Total/Average	-				$	-	**#DIV/0!**

Figure 13.5   *The Executive Dashboard summarizes data from the Marketing Channel Dashboard*

Now that you have the framework for your reporting dashboard, it will be much easier to produce reports for yourself and your management team. The measurement tools reviewed in Chapter 11, "Measurement Tool Review," will make collecting this data super easy. You'll simply log in, pull the metrics from your measurement tool dashboard, and then plug them into your Excel dashboard. If you spent the time to connect all your formulas in Excel, it will auto-calculate all your summary data and even update your executive report automatically. It's also best to include a simple summary report of key insights you've found, such as the ones in the following example.

Key Points

Social media represented 1% of the total budget and led to the following results:

- Social media supported brand awareness efforts by generating a 186% lift in total impressions.
- Social media led to a 33% decrease in total cost per impression.
- Social media led to an 99% decrease in total cost per engagement.
- Social media generated an 88% decrease in total cost per site visit.
- Social media improved brand awareness efforts by generating close to 500,000 different forms of engagement from the audience.

Don't expect executives to interpret the data for you. Make it easy for them to see the value.

Eventually, there will be a measurement tool that has these reports built into its dashboards to completely automate the process. Until then, it's up to you to make sure you're reporting on the data that executives care about. Don't let your desire for a perfect tool get in the way of proving social media's value.

Hands-On Exercise: Build Your Dashboard

Set Up One of the Most Important Meetings You've Had on Your Calendar in Weeks

Attendees: You, Your Computer, and Excel

Seriously, put four hours on your calendar right now to build your own dashboard. Yes, realistically, it will take that long. But it will be the most productive four hours you've spent on social media since you built out your measurable strategies at the beginning of the book. When your calendar alert pops up to remind you it's time to build your dashboard, come back and follow these step-by-step instructions.

## 14

Tying It All Together

It's time to stop making social media return on investment (ROI) so hard. It's tangible. It can be measured using the tips throughout this book. But getting there takes a different approach. Lose the fluff and stop trying to treat social media marketing like it deserves its own pedestal in your organization. Your executives won't buy that approach for long, and you'll be setting yourself up for failure. If you do your job well, social media soon will be fully integrated into business and marketing activities and as common as email marketing. Remember the battles you faced selling email marketing through the organization? The arguments about invading privacy and annoying customers? But at the end of the day the naysayers stepped aside, and robust email marketing strategies and campaigns took their rightful place in the marketing mix. Although similar arguments about social media are starting to dissipate, and executives are optimistic, they're also cautious. They aren't handing out huge budgets for marketers to go out and test what will work. Rather, executives want to see the ROI before they'll invest money that looks anything like what they invest in other marketing channels. Marketers are stuck with a true chicken-and-egg scenario: Proving out the ROI is difficult, although not impossible, when you can't invest in truly integrated strategy and campaign development.

Unfortunately, you probably are your own worst enemy. Your executives are asking for ROI, and you're showing them social metrics like fans, followers, retweets, likes, and shares—all of which are difficult to correlate to the bottom line. Marketers are still attributing arbitrary "conversion values" that have no true correlation to real revenue for the conversions they create. Stop. Instead, take this opportunity to demonstrate your understanding of business and business objectives—and make every report easy for an executive to understand. The three metrics that every executive understands, and uses, are sales volume, revenue, and cost. Correlate social media's impact on those key metrics, and your executive team will start to understand its contribution to the overall health of the organization. Getting at sales volume and revenue may take some work, depending on how your company stores the data, but absolutely start measuring social media's effect on costs *right now*. You have no excuse.

To deliver results, social media strategies need to be measureable, and they need to align with business objectives. What are the business's core goals—the ones that sales and customer service teams are being measured against? What's the focus of the five-year growth plan—selling more units or hours, increasing profitability, cutting expenses, raising prices, or getting customers to buy more? Whatever those core objectives are, it's time to align your social media strategy to at least one of them.

When a strategy isn't designed to deliver on a specific goal, it's likely to result in a lot of good "ideas" with little chance of actually making an impact on the bottom line. It isn't because they're bad ideas; it's because the idea wasn't created with the end result in mind. The time to throw ideas against the wall to see what sticks isn't when an executive is pressing for ROI. So it's important to evaluate your efforts to see if they fit with your new perspective on where social media fits into the sales funnel, which marketing goals they're best suited to impact, and which business objective you're going to focus on affecting.

Now that you know what you are trying to accomplish and have done the exercises to determine how you will accomplish it, it's time to start measuring. You can invest in sophisticated tools, or you can start with something simple you could implement today without large budget approvals. Either choice will get you better data than you have today, so don't wait. Get a solution in place next week. It's a waste of time doing an in-depth analysis if you don't have metrics. At a minimum, use HootSuite and Google Analytics while you do your in-depth analysis if your company requires it. It's unacceptable to put this book down and not have an immediate plan to implement a measurement solution, even if it is just short-term while you build toward perfection.

This book is based on 14 years of sitting in executive meetings at companies of all sizes trying to get budget approval for this idea or that idea. After years of success and failures, it became clear that the key to winning in the boardroom is to stop trying to change the executives. Instead, change your approach to be in line with what executives want. You need to understand how their brains work, what they care about, how they evaluate ideas and, most importantly, what factors they use to make decisions. Then you can structure presentations around those factors, giving executives answers to their questions before they even ask them. This will take time, and you won't get it right the first time. But every time you do a presentation, you'll learn something you can adjust the next time.

Although each executive is unique, one thing is consistent: The board of directors measures the success of an executive by the financial health of the company. In a small company, where there isn't a board of directors, the buck stops at the CEO or company's owners. They didn't go into business to lose money. Even nonprofit organizations need to raise revenue to fund new programs and initiatives.

Your job is to make your executive team look like super stars who hired a talented group of individuals who are getting the job done. If you're successful, you may find that your executive team looks at you a little differently. A lot of marketers would struggle as corporate executives, so when those executives see someone who delivers results and understands their goals, it isn't uncommon for them to start building that person into their succession plans. The succession plan is what the company uses to groom people for senior-level positions. You want your name on that plan. And the quickest way to get there is to start making yourself an indispensible part of the team—showing that you understand business and happen to have a competence for marketing, as well. Demonstrating that you can build a strategy to solve business problems, successfully implement it, and measure your impact along the way is key to your long-term success in any organization. And if your goal is to make it into senior positions, it will be equally important to prove that you can teach others to do the same. It doesn't matter what level your position is in the organization; every company is looking for the right talent to groom. Be that talent. Play it to win it.

Hands-On Exercise: Social Media ROI Assessment

The general assessment in Figure 14.1 will help you see what you need to focus on to take your social media strategy to the next level. If you score a little low, don't get discouraged. Most companies are still at the early adopter stage and score 20 points or less. This doesn't mean you aren't doing some great things. It just means there's an opportunity to focus your efforts on addressing some of the items you answered "No" to, so that you can start truly delivering social media ROI.

social media explorer

SOCIAL MEDIA ROI ASSESSMENT

Item	Yes	No	Notes	Points for Yes Response	Your Score
Does your company have a clearly defined target audience for your products/services?			List target audiences	1	
Has your company identified any "niche" audiences as high priority targets?			List niche audiences	1	
Does your company have clear goals for this year in terms of revenue, profitability and expenses?			List general goals	5	
Is your company interested in generating more leads online?			Rank the priority of the next three ?s. Priority 1, 2, 3	2	
Is your company interested in generating more revenue from existing customers?			Priority 1, 2, 3	2	
Is your company interested in generating more brand awareness for your company with your target markets?			Priority 1, 2, 3	2	
Has your company optimized the path to conversion from the social channel?				8	
Are you currently trying to achieve one of these goals with social media?			List which goal is being pursued with social media.	2	
Do you have executive buy-in for social media?				3	
Do you have a social media strategy in place?				7	
If yes, does your strategy align with the achievement of corporate goals?			List goals	10	
Do you have a specific and defined goal for each social network you are participating in?			List goals	12	
Do you have a content strategy that drives the decision making process to buy your products or service?				10	
Do you have a content calendar that enables you to create content 30, 60, 90 days in advance?				10	
Can you measure the success of your social media efforts in terms of impact on sales volume, revenue and cost?				10	
Can you identify which of your social media tactics is delivering the highest return?				10	
Do you have personnel assigned to social media efforts?			_____ people	2	
			Dedicated to SM? Y or N	3	

Score				Points Possible	Your Score
				100	

Figure 14.1 *Social media ROI assessment*

Index

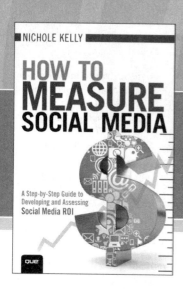

NICHOLE KELLY

HOW TO MEASURE SOCIAL MEDIA

A Step-by-Step Guide to Developing and Assessing Social Media ROI

que

FREE
Online Edition

Safari
Books Online

Your purchase of *How to Measure Social Media* includes access to a free online edition for 45 days through the **Safari Books Online** subscription service. Nearly every Que book is available online through **Safari Books Online**, along with thousands of books and videos from publishers such as Addison-Wesley Professional, Cisco Press, Exam Cram, IBM Press, O'Reilly Media, Prentice Hall, and Sams.

Safari Books Online is a digital library providing searchable, on-demand access to thousands of technology, digital media, and professional development books and videos from leading publishers. With one monthly or yearly subscription price, you get unlimited access to learning tools and information on topics including mobile app and software development, tips and tricks on using your favorite gadgets, networking, project management, graphic design, and much more.

Activate your FREE Online Edition at
informit.com/safarifree

STEP 1: Enter the coupon code: OUPOLCB.

STEP 2: New Safari users, complete the brief registration form.
Safari subscribers, just log in.

If you have difficulty registering on Safari or accessing the online edition,
please e-mail customer-service@safaribooksonline.com